Bramble Rambles

Bob Ford

an imprint of Sunbury Press, Inc.
Mechanicsburg, PA USA

an imprint of Sunbury Press, Inc.
Mechanicsburg, PA USA

Copyright © 2022 by Bob Ford.
Cover Copyright © 2022 by Sunbury Press, Inc.

Sunbury Press supports copyright. Copyright fuels creativity, encourages diverse voices, promotes free speech, and creates a vibrant culture. Thank you for buying an authorized edition of this book and for complying with copyright laws by not reproducing, scanning, or distributing any part of it in any form without permission. You are supporting writers and allowing Sunbury Press to continue to publish books for every reader. For information contact Sunbury Press, Inc., Subsidiary Rights Dept., PO Box 548, Boiling Springs, PA 17007 USA or legal@sunburypress.com.

For information about special discounts for bulk purchases, please contact Sunbury Press Orders Dept. at (855) 338-8359 or orders@sunburypress.com.

To request one of our authors for speaking engagements or book signings, please contact Sunbury Press Publicity Dept. at publicity@sunburypress.com.

FIRST SCRIPTORIA PRESS EDITION: December 2022

Set in Adobe Garamond Pro | Interior design by Crystal Devine | Cover by Lawrence Knorr | Edited by Lawrence Knorr.

Publisher's Cataloging-in-Publication Data
Names: Ford, Bob, author.
Title: Bramble rambles / Bob Ford.
Description: First trade paperback edition. | Mechanicsburg, PA : Scriptoria Press, 2022.
Summary: Reverend Bob Ford, renowned sportsman, shares his Christian thoughts inspired by his many jaunts into the brush with his beagles.
Identifiers: ISBN 979-8-88819-022-7 (softcover) | ISBN 979-8-88819-023-4 (ePub).
Subjects: RELIGION / Christian Living / Personal Memoirs | RELIGION / Christian Living / Spiritual Growth | RELIGION / Christian Ministry / Preaching.

Product of the United States of America
0 1 1 2 3 5 8 13 21 34 55

Continue the Enlightenment!

Introduction

I call these short reflections "rambles," but they are probably a bit more organized. Originally, they all appeared as social media posts to promote more positivity in a place that can be mean-spirited. I call them "bramble" because they were mostly written while outside enjoying nature with my dogs. Well, the thoughts occurred there; I often wrote these reflections after finishing an early morning ramble (walk) in the brambles. Some of the content comes from sources I cite, other notions are commonplace, and sometimes I will quote a source, though this is not intended to be an academic exercise. Rather, I hope each small chapter is a place to initiate conversations amongst believers as we work through serious issues of faith as we interact in the contemporary world and navigate the waters of how we walk with faith while incorporating our intellectual struggle to make sense of things that are best addressed in the community. In that respect, these chapters are not answers. Just a place to launch dialogue as sojourners in our time and our place.

Prayerful Dance

There's this tendency in Christianity to gravitate towards simplistic platitudes. You know them.

God is good all the time. All the time, God is good. Frog—Fully Rely On God. WWJD, or What Would Jesus Do? That one always gets me since there are many opinions about who the earthly Jesus was while sojourning in the flesh. Jesus, like the Bible, can be used to say what we want, even if that interpretation isn't faithful to the ministry of Jesus.

What we do know Jesus frequently did was pray. After The Last Supper, Luke tells us that Jesus goes to the Mount of Olives (as usual, he says) to pray. Jesus prays all the time in the Gospels. Jesus is fully God, but because he is fully human, he prays. I've heard atheistic jokes about how if Jesus is divine, he must be talking to himself when he prayed. But Jesus prayed a lot. The Godhead (Father, Son, and Holy Ghost) is often portrayed in static ways. Shamrock. The trinity knot (you can Google it) or a triangle.

For me, the trinity is much more dynamic. Like when you see three siblings or friends that are so close, they can all talk at once, and they are all following what is being said. Somehow. As an outsider, we watch that dynamism and are confused. Jesus prays because it is his nature. The Word of God, The Son, necessarily is in a dynamic relationship with the Father and The Spirit. Put the shamrock aside and picture an atom with whirling orbits. Father, Son, and Spirit orbit each other in dynamism. I will come back to this . . .

Jesus is a praying presence. We routinely find ourselves baffled, perhaps trying to troubleshoot a mechanical glitch in a car, correct a child, persuade an aging parent about how their medications have changed, or try to get the Wifi to work and say some odd phrase akin to "I've tried everything but pray."

That almost sets up prayer as the next thing to fail. The car doesn't start. It seems to have gas. It has spark. It has air. Those aren't the problem. I prayed. It is still not working.

Ahh, and if we pray and pray and then pray some more and do not get what we want, what do we say? I can tell you what people say—God didn't answer my prayer. I changed the plugs and the fuel pump, and nothing helped. Prayer failed too.

This puts prayer in a toolbox. Right next to the screwdriver and the wrenches. Or right next to the measuring cups and the cooking knives. Or on your resume, next to your education and experience. With your skills (Typing, shorthand, prayer . . .). That makes prayer mine. Frames it in relationship to me.

But that Trinitarian Godhead is a whirling, dynamic thing. What prayer does is scoop us up into the movement. Prayer inserts all of us into that mystery. We are all in this movement. Let's call it a dance. Like the most complicated line dance you ever saw. Or a square dance. Even more complicated than those, actually.

Imagine one of those choreographed dances with a high aerial camera for you to see the complexities of the dance. The tempo changes in the music. None of the dancers can see the whole thing. They are too enmeshed in their parts. At most, they can feel the dance and be assured that it is going properly because the song is still going and they are still making the right moves.

Prayer puts us in the dance, and we are communing with the Godhead. It isn't a tool like the dancing shoes, the big belt buckle if you are line dancing or the boots. Prayer isn't what we have; it is what we do.

Bramble Rambles

It is how we move. The rest of the world may not get it. If you watch a musical, do you ever think, "Who breaks into song and dance like that?" I think that all the time when my wife watches a miracle. The world doesn't understand the dance any more than I understand *Grease* when Renee watches it.

When you are getting up for the day, fixing breakfast for the kids, getting them to school, and then going to work while checking on doctor appointments for your aging parents and organizing a fundraiser at school—you are in the dance. That is the dance where the prayer happens, not just when we close our eyes and bow our heads. If we do it well, we bring others into the dance.

Remember, it is communication like those three siblings talking at once. Prayer is not a wish list or a magic trick. It is the most profound communication, giving our words to The Word and listening back. Prayer doesn't fail. When Jesus went to the Garden to pray, Matthew tells us that Jesus prayed for the cup to pass if possible. Just a few minutes later, he is arrested, and the long torture of his execution begins. He didn't get what he asked for. And we do not always get what we ask. We can't see the whole dance, just like the full humanity of Jesus prevented him from seeing it all, too, despite his full divinity. Keep on dancing.

Punishment

"**God must be** punishing me for something," I heard in a waiting room yesterday. Now, the fact that I post stuff on here, and do public speaking every Sunday, might give you the impression that I'm an extrovert. Not at all, not naturally. But I can function in public. Typically, I'd ignore people I'm listening to in a waiting room. But, this notion that God is some sort of sadist looking to punish us, like a demented college fraternity president trying to haze us until we make it to heaven, is a mindset that I think is way too prevalent and causes way too much anguish. So, I talked to the guy who got laid off and forgot to get gasoline, and his car was down to a quarter tank, and he was in the waiting room waiting for his aging father, who was just getting a check-up and doing well health-wise. Getting laid off is no bowl of cherries, but given the context of the conversation (hospital) and his dad's good prognosis, I thought he was doing okay. He was starting a new job in a week.

Looking at our circumstances—where we work, what we make, how much gasoline the car has—as indicators of God's retribution or blessing is an odd game. So, does Divine punishment exist? If so, how do we see it? You read about criminals in the paper who have no sense of guilt. No remorse. They only get caught by human law enforcement. They aren't going to have a change of heart on their own. Doesn't appear to be any punishment from God. Biblically, it seems that punishment is something

God reserves for His people more often than not. Not the outsiders. I'm not saying that's always the case (Pharaoh, for example).

But if God punishes us, it's because He loves us. I knew a guy who bought a beagle from a place constantly selling pups and adult dogs. This dog was one year old and AKC-registered, so it certainly had a name. This guy bought the dog because its pedigree was solid red—five generations of field champions.

The owner wanted to solo the dog. Despite having a name, it is clear that the dog doesn't know it. It's clear that the dog doesn't know "Come here," or "Down," or any basic command we might teach. The dog runs a rabbit. Loses it. The guy starts calling the dog. Does it come? No. Proof that some guys ought not to have E-collars, he zaps the dog. He uses the damn thing like I use my microwave—highest setting only.

The dog runs from the pain—away from the owner. Gets another high zap and runs in another direction. Zap. The dog is smart, which is good because I'm about to lose my noggin. It comes and sits at its new owner's feet. Maybe the puppy mill was better. This guy thinks he has taught the dog "Here," but, in fact, it's a smart dog that figured out that if it ventured away from his new owner, it hurt. In other words, you can't use an E-collar to teach a command. It can only reinforce something that the dog already knows. That pedigreed pooch didn't even know his name.

I use collars. Mostly I use the GPS function. I zap myself with any collar so that I know how high each setting is. My dogs don't need much. Ever stick a 9-volt battery on your tongue? It takes less than that. Actually, it takes way less. I have a button that makes a beeping tone. The dog has to ignore that two or three times before it gets the mild nip. When would I use the shock? To keep the dog safe. Don't chase a deer. Guys shoot dogs for that (though here in Pennsylvania, they can't legally shoot your dog unless it is attacking the deer). If we get too close to a hardtop road looking for a rabbit, and I move in another direction, I call "here," and if the dog doesn't come, I use the beeping tone. Mostly, I use my collars for the GPS function. I can see right where they are. I don't use the E-collar function much at all. And that is almost always a tone. A beep. No pain. Because my dogs know the commands already.

How much more can we learn as people rather than as dogs? We can talk. We can teach our kids. We can learn throughout our lives. When we feel reservations about doing something as a believer, that is a tone. When we do something wrong, that is a shock. We then correct our behavior because the point isn't pain; it protects us from going towards the road.

This is how I see divine punishment. Not as oppressive pain but as corrective measures rooted in compassion and love, intended to keep us safe. Sometimes we know people who never seem to feel forgiven. There are times I think that is due to the person having hang-ups of their own. But, I think we often find that people who feel guilty even when forgiven are like that poor dog I saw that day. He was punished and never knew why. Once he stayed close, the guy was going to shock to get him to start hunting again. Can you imagine the confusion for that dog? I stopped him. He says he was mad at me because he's owned dogs longer than me.

There are kids raised in homes with random punishment in many forms (spanking, verbal yelling, being ignored . . .), and there is no rhyme, reason, or consistency to these punishments. Or very little. Like that dog. Then, that life experience gets packed up as an adult and becomes the baggage brought to our understanding of how we interact with our Heavenly Father. That poor dog has an uphill battle, but those believers who respond to tone can help a new dog in the pack. A good pack helps a new hound as much as any other training. Let's be good packmates.

Problems with Reduction

$$C8H11NO2+C10H12N2O+C43H66N12O12S2$$

That's the chemical formula for love. It's dopamine, serotonin, and oxytocin. They can make it in a lab, and overdosing can make you schizophrenic and paranoid and cause other mental anguish. It's the chemical flood that happens when we fall in love. The biology of it.

Is anyone going to sign a valentine with that formula instead of the word love? It refers to erotic or romantic love. The biochemical impetus for human reproduction. But, even in terms of romantic love, it doesn't tell the whole story. The first parish I ever served, while I was still in seminary, had five couples who together were celebrating 319 years of marriage—farmers who married young and then had the blessing of longevity.

They were past the lustful years—beyond the hormonal definition of attraction. They were into those years when they knew each other so well that they could virtually communicate without language. Just look at each other. Reductionism. That is the process of reducing a very complex thing into a simple statement, like using 155 mph to describe the experience of being in a muscle car hustling down the highway. That happened to me once—155 mph doesn't come close to describing what it was like in the passenger seat of that Mustang on a two-lane road with a guy trying to scare the pastor as we hurtled along a narrow road that crossed the Pennsylvania/New York border in the twin tiers. Or, maybe you could define the feeling of walking into a warm house on a cold night and describing the fireplace in terms of BTUs and ambient room temperature. I mean, you could do that, but there are better ways of defining what it means to come home after a long day and feel the warmth as you slump into your favorite chair and welcome the weight of a beagle on your lap as you twirl his long ears in a way that they warm your cool hands.

When we talk about the Love of God, agape, and the love of ethics, we are talking about a transformative love that cascades into the world and makes all things new. It isn't a cocktail of biochemistry. Formulas. Equations. Sports scores. Abbreviated jargon utilized in text messages like BRB LMAO LOL IDK. Emojis that are even less thorough. Memes. Reductionism run amok, I tell you. We are living short form.

TLTR. Too long to read. It typifies a world swamped with information but mostly willing to read no more than two scrolls. Short answers are preferred, even if they are inherently inaccurate. Complex policy in the world of politics is reduced to sound bites. I've always liked songs that were too long for FM radio. Rush's "2112" is one. It is over 20 minutes long. It is not good for radio; they need commercials and advertising dollars.

Long conversations on complex topics are sorely lacking. I know people who take more time to describe the dessert they ate than they use to explain a philosophy of life to their kids. Tonight, after supper, unplug the modem. Then hide it. Then let the conversation be anything but reduced. Let it be complex, with tangents and sidetracks, and then look for the interactions of those sidetracks, and then see that there can be a system that seems to incorporate all these things, and that system is much more than the sum of the parts.

Tale of Two Testaments

When I was a kid and into adulthood, Western Auto and Sears were common stores. Western Auto carried all kinds of stuff, including hunting gear. Small towns would have a catalog store for their Sears. You would order something, then go back in a week or so and pick it up. I'm not sure if all the Sears are gone now, but I've seen a bunch disappear. I haven't seen a Western Auto in a very long time. Know what I see? Dollar General and Walmart. The whole world has gone to cheap and disposable. It's tougher and tougher to find clothes or boots that last. My mom said the only shoes I always outgrew as a kid were Sears canvas sneakers.

Sometimes I get nostalgic for days when they repaired televisions that only had four channels, and there were plenty of places to get new soles put on your shoes. "The Good Old Days" mentality. In the Middle Ages, following Rome's collapse, people looked back at the old days as better. There was a lot of knowledge lost for centuries. The Renaissance was all about discovering lost information. In Protestant circles, there was a return to biblical languages. That meant Greek for the New Testament and Hebrew for the Old Testament.

The earliest Gentile Christians did not use the Hebrew Old Testament. It was a Greek translation called the Septuagint. That was the holy scripture for many Jewish people scattered throughout the Mediterranean and beyond. If at the time of Jesus, you could speak Greek and Latin, you could walk from Israel to England, and if you kept to the cities, you could get by anywhere. Kind of like English is today. Today, when people from opposite ends of Europe meet, English is often the common language.

Anyway, Protestants flocked to Hebrew. Latin was all the rage, and the church had translated the Septuagint and the New Testament into Latin. That was the Bible in Europe; unless you were Orthodox, then you had the Greek. Protestants went right to the Hebrew. As a result, they changed their Old Testament to the same as the Jewish Bible. It has fewer books. That's why Catholic and Orthodox Bibles have more books. Protestants dropped anything that was not utilized in the Jewish community.

Now, the oldest Hebrew Bibles are from the years 935 and 1008. Middle Ages. The oldest Greek Septuagint stuff goes back to the 3rd century BC. The big brains argue about which is more genuine. Does older mean more original? The short answer is not really. But using those extra Old Testament books was our earliest practice. Some of them get referenced in the New Testament. "Desolating sacrilege" is straight out of Maccabees. Neither 1 or 2 Maccabees makes the Jewish Bible, but the events tell the story central to Hanukkah.

So, I like to read both. If the New Testament is quoting the Old Testament, you can bet that the Greek Septuagint is being quoted. Often verbatim. Jesus spoke Aramaic, which is hinted at when he speaks from the cross, "*Eloi eloi lamma sabachthani*" or "My Lord my Lord, why have you forsaken me?" The truth, however, is that the Gospel writers have Jesus and all the others speaking Greek. And they probably didn't.

So, read all the versions and variations. When I was young, the differences bothered me. I somehow thought that truth required complete congruence across the board. But that kind of emphasis on literal truth, I think, reduces truth to facticity. I'm convinced God inspired the Bible. I'm not sure all of the human authors knew that they were writing sacred scriptures. I think if Paul knew he would get more books in the Bible than anyone, he would have been more . . . polite and precise. So, I think the believers who hand-copied for centuries knew they were preserving God's word, but I'm not sure all the original authors did.

And that's okay with me. Lots of believers would disagree with me. That's okay with me too. I'm not going to tell them they are not Christians. We are just of different opinions of what it means for the Scriptures to be the inspired word of God. To be honest, there is an extreme similarity in the various bibles, and much of the differences are article (like a/an/the in English) variations. Certainly, there are larger variations too.

But, and this is where I have been headed, Jesus spoke Aramaic, a variation of Hebrew, but his teaching is preserved in Greek. If I limit truth to literal words and memorize verses (in King James, of course) that I can hurl at someone in a debate, then I have chosen a smaller truth. In fact, it might violate the Bible. That command about not having idols. If we aren't careful, we turn the Bible into an idol. An idol, of course, is a representation of something. The pagans didn't really worship statues. They just had statues to represent their gods. If we aren't careful, we can turn The Word of God into an idol called the Bible.

Reading Job Is a Tough Job

We are getting some weather today, so my mind turns to the book of Job. Job is a very long book, and if you have one of those parallel bibles, you will see many variations in translations—because it is old. Some of the oldest writing we have. So the big brains have to decide on certain arcane words and phrases. Anyway, it is old because it addresses a universal topic—suffering—why some do and others do not, and how ethics are irrelevant. Behaving or misbehaving doesn't matter in this life as a predictor of who will have tragedy, sickness, or death touch their lives.

Where was I? Oh, the weather. For 37 chapters Job and his buddies are in dialogue about why Job is suffering. Popular thinking at that time was that living well brought blessings, and living wickedly brought retribution. We know, however, that the wicked often thrive, and the faithful seem to be living a life like running a gauntlet of doom and despair. Job did not deserve his plight. In chapter 38, God speaks to Job—rather rudely. And, to oversimplify, the answer that God gives is, "I created the universe, and you did not." And the passage then reveals the Hebraic understanding of the physical world. It talks about storehouses for snow and hail. Rain, too, as blocked by clouds. It is almost like the world (flat) has an invisible dome over it. The invisible dome has doors, or gates, that can be opened, and rain might fall. Or, like today, snow. It is quaint, to be sure, but the overall imagery points to order. One that is too complex for people to see. Chapter 39 continues with the complexities of the living creatures of this world, their various gestation times, how they survive, and the natural order.

The idea of gates that let weather fall to the ground isn't accurate, but neither is telling our kids that thunder is "God bowling" in heaven. Does anyone else get told that as a youngster? And, I don't think if we told the author of Job that the world is round and the only thing akin to a dome is the actual atmosphere, which is complex beyond belief—well, I don't know that this information would be a problem for the author of Job. A complex world that only God fully fathoms is just what the book of Job says is the way things are. Like when meteorologists give forecasts, we still find a day like this with roads that are more treacherous than predicted and commutes that are way more hazardous than we thought when we went to bed.

That's the only answer Job ever gets. Creation is beyond our full knowledge, and shut up. Not real comforting, is it? All we really get from Job is the certainty that what we get in life isn't justice. Our physical state doesn't necessarily provide a readout of our ethical ledger. You can be a paragon of moral virtue and be stricken with a nasty thing like ALS or pancreatic cancer. You can be the most selfish person alive and enjoy longevity, health, and wealth.

That, to me, is the challenge of Job. Why be moral? We, of course, will point to the afterlife and the promises of resurrection for the faithful. Job lived centuries before anyone knew anything about the resurrection or life everlasting. Job lived in a world where you died, which was a shadowy nothing in Sheol, no matter how you lived. So, that's the power of Job for me. It asserts ethics and morality while also saying there is no guarantee living properly will benefit you. Somehow, morality is part of creation and what it means to be human. Doing the right thing is never about benefit to self, but rather it is a divine mystery. Why do some people behave with compassion and kindness, and others rarely do?

Bramble Rambles

Job is old. There is some newish stuff in there, though. I mean, it is still ancient, but not as ancient as the rest of the book, so the scholars have determined. It is the part where Job gets everything back and goes about being wealthy and healthy again. There is just something about the randomness of suffering that perhaps sat wrong with some people at the time, as it does now. Doing the right thing no matter what it gets you has never been popular.

These are just my thoughts as I watch the storehouses of snow open. Every dang snowflake is completely different than any other one that has ever fallen to the ground or will ever fall to the ground. And righteousness exists even when it is not rewarded.

Magnets and Missing

The Greek word for sin is *amartia*. It can be found in many instances to mean "miss the mark," as in archery when an arrow misses. As a hunter, missing is one thing that bugs me the most. When I am rabbit hunting, I will let the bunny keep circling until I can get a good shot, one I can make and one that will not damage the meat. I never take a shot at a rabbit running away from me.

Missing is never fun. If you are not a hunter, perhaps you are a sports fan. A batter in baseball can fail seventy percent of the time and be one of the best players in the game. There's a lot of missing, even when doing well. I know college kids who Uber or Lyft around campus and the surrounding town while studying at Penn State. I remember taking the bus. There was nothing worse than approaching the bus stop and seeing it pull away; it would be another wait for the next bus. Missing the bus was bad, though I often only used it when it rained.

The notion of missing the mark implies taking a shot. Doing something. Sometimes, when I sin, it is trying to make the shot and not connecting. I am trying to do the right thing, which turns out wrong. I have the best intentions—a joke, intended to be light-hearted and fun, lands wrong, and what I say turns out to be mean. Those sins I do unintentionally by "missing the mark" while attempting to do positive things bother me.

Bob Ford

What bothers me more are the misses that occur because I deliberately miss because I am aiming at the wrong target. I hit what I wanted, but it was not the proper target. I've been known to say mean things that aren't even attempted humor. I just hurt someone's feelings because we are on opposite sides of an issue. I might be in the woods and just come home late, on purpose, because the dogs are doing particularly well that day. I know my wife is making supper, but I also know that there is no way to know when it will be done. It all depends on when she started. Sometimes I get home late, and it is still not done—no biggie. Sometimes I make her wait. You know what? She has this dang pressure cooker now, which is seldom late. I still act like it will be. I do it on purpose. Those are the misses that really irk me. The ones I do on purpose, knowing they are wrong.

But, I can honestly say those incidents get less frequent over time. No doubt. The term Christian was an insult when it emerged. Outsiders called us that. It means "Little Christs" or something like that. And that is exactly what we are called to be. I remember in elementary school, I had these magnets in my desk. I liked playing with them on my desk when I was done with my work during those times when it was unstructured work time. I liked to line up the poles north to north or south to south and push the magnets across the desktop without touching them. Sometimes I would make a maze and try to steer the magnet through it.

At any rate, I left a paper clip on this big magnet the whole year. When I took my magnets home at the end of the year, I discovered that the paper clip had become a small magnet. It was strong enough to pick up another paper clip. But, when left off the magnet, it ceased to be one. It demagnetized just from storing it in a drawer, away from the magnet. That's the way it is with my missing the mark. It gets better over time so long as I am in contact with Christ. I am a Christian to Christ, like that paper clip on a magnet. I find that if I do not take time to be with Christ—and it happens—especially if I am busy and driving all over the place for hospital visits and meetings, then I tend to miss more. I begin to demagnetize. The strongest Christians spend the most time with Christ.

Love and Marriage

Chocolate and flowers are everywhere around Valentine's Day. It wasn't until Chaucer that the day gained ground as being about romantic love. Scholars often tell us that marriage was not about romance in antiquity. *Oikos* is Greek for house. And it is the root of economics. The base unit of the ancient economies was the household. Everyone worked. Often at home. Kids too. Kids were your retirement in a world without pensions or social security. That commandment about honoring our mother and father is all about taking care of them in old age. It's not about little kids behaving.

Anyway, marriage was the foundation of the family, and the family was the basic unit of commerce. Commuting to work wasn't too far. Especially in an agrarian world, most people did not live in a city. People lived close to the land. Adultery was a sin, not just a sexual sin, but a societal problem that could really disrupt things in terms of inheritance, land in particular, if children resulted from the affair. Living with a small house and a tiny yard is easy today, but it hasn't been all that long since real wealth was understood as land and the food it produced.

But there is erotic/romantic stuff in the Bible. A whole book of poems called Song of Songs. It's odd that, like the book of Esther, it never mentions God. Well, the Hebrew version of Esther doesn't mention God. The longer Greek version does and is used in the Bible by Roman Catholic brothers and sisters. Song of Songs can be pretty . . . well, sexual. A man and a woman exchange dialogue in these poems. They aren't dirty limericks but rather a celebration of love. There was an old tradition that a single person was only half a person. It took the complimentary bond with the opposite sex to bring fulfillment.

My wife and I had a passage from Song of Songs read as the scripture at our wedding. It's a book that celebrates romantic love. The whole book. Some wonder how it made the cut to be in the Bible. It had to be popular to get in there without mentioning God even once. The prevailing interpretation is that it is an allegory for love between God and his people. The most intimate human interaction is analogous to God's love for us.

Actually, divine love may be more intimate. It's amazing how many couples with several children, as proof of their intimacy, have never prayed together. Prayer is an extraordinarily intimate act. Not sexual, but that's the closest analogy. People get worked up over Valentine's Day. Depressed if single. They look for the perfect gift and meal if they have a significant other. The New Testament has plenty of emphasis on living single. Jesus did. Paul says we can marry if we have to if we need to have an outlet for sexual needs. Not a real high endorsement of marriage. What I'm getting at is that it's okay to be married or single. Francis Asbury, an early bishop of American Methodism, preferred single pastors. They could get more work done. I often hear the same argument for celibate priests. They aren't burdened by family. I view family as a blessing, not a burden. I think married pastors understand family dynamics better, though not all do. And some single clergy are great at understanding families.

Single or married, we are called to agape. Eros is erotic love. Agape is love in action, changing the world for the better. It's the love read at most weddings. 1 Corinthians 13. It's famous, and you can look it up easy. It's a powerful mandate for kindness, patience, humility, and more. And it's how we ought to treat everyone, not just our spouse! It's a high standard, and it's how a believer interacts with people. Take a gander at 1 Corinthians 13. It's who we are. I guess I better figure out where to take my wife to eat for Valentine's Day. Would she be happy if I just cooked a pot of rabbit stew?

Liberal and Conservative

I'll take the adjectives of liberal and conservative (often insults from the other side, or traditional and progressive (terms sometimes self-claimed) and look at them a bit. I remember when the terms were two poles with a very long spectrum. There was a center, of course, but what was more important was that there was a spectrum. A spectrum that could be traversed. And so, you could embrace a host of ideas, some conservative and others liberal. People could pick a la carte and not buy a package deal.

Imagine that spectrum as a flat field—maybe like a football field, a big thing today. Then suppose that we were all standing on that field. And imagine if the center (50-yard line) were raised. And it kept being raised. Higher and higher. Until it was so steep that it was a sheer face, no one could stand in the center. The poles were left. The extreme views. But those of us accustomed to a la carte life were left with far left and far right. What do you do? If you were a centrist a bit right of center, you might have been forced to the far right, or vice versa. The extreme view of the other side is essentially the worst of two evils, and the extreme on our side is the lesser evil. Sound familiar?

I should have put this as an initial disclaimer, but I've decided to save it until now. I am not talking about politics. It's everywhere. As a Christian and a pastor, I've gathered insight from the whole spectrum.

Bob Ford

I'm a big proponent of modern biblical scholarship, comparative study of religions, and ancient cultural contexts. In other words, I'm not a guy that reads every word of the Bible literally. Some stories contradict others; poetry is never meant to be literal, I think the world is older than 5,000 years, and there is always a danger of turning the Word into an idol. Some of my brothers and sisters would call me a liberal here.

But I'm an evangelical. The kind that believes in a personal encounter with Christ. At my ordination vows, I affirmed a belief in Christian perfection as espoused by Wesley (I agonized over it. I have colleagues who just made the public statement despite not believing it), and I truly believe in that radical grace. The doctrine can be oversimplified as meaning that we can and ought to get to a place where everything we do is motivated by the love of God and the love of our neighbor. We still sin by accident or lack of insight. But not intentionally. I'm not there yet, but I've known people I think were/are. They'd never claim it, though. It's a perfection of love that leaves no room for that kind of pride, I think.

Anyway, that's pretty conservative, and I was all in on the concept before I got out of seminary. Lying about your assent to the question seemed an odd way to start life as an ordained pastor, so I refused to do that. I teach and preach the radical, transformative concept of grace in my tradition. I'm all for helping people and outreach—even if it helps people who are not yet Christian. If we go to the most difficult places and build hospitals and schools, that will be a more effective sermon than anything else. It will save lives, and some will no doubt be converted. For some Christians, this is a very liberal idea. Our local community stopped doing crop walk a decade ago because some of the money went overseas to feed people who did not have to convert or pray to Christ before being fed. That's too right for me.

That being said, I'm pretty conservative in my view that Christ is the way. Just because I feel we are called to help others no matter what doesn't mean I'm not working for Christ. Or that I think all religions are equal paths to get to God. Why would I be a pastor if I felt beliefs didn't matter? I'm not saying I know who is saved and who is not, but some labeled me pretty conservative for being solidly in that Jesus camp.

But increasingly, as the center is lifted, what really happens is that it goes away. We are left with two end zones. But nobody is trying to get to the other one. So I ask: Who benefits from a world with no center or spectrum? Just two poles. What is the benefit of diametric, antagonistic, often pugilistic poles? Is there a handful of people at the steep peak, reaping all the benefits? $5.6 million for a 30-second commercial likes just two sides. Coke or Pepsi. Ford or Chevy. Is it something more dangerous? Human nature hell-bent on inflicting not just vitriolic speech but ultimately hate and violence?

Maybe the center could return. And be a conduit that can channel evangelism and outreach. Promote scripture and grace. A spectrum could come back so we can walk from end to end and benefit from others. I'm comfortable standing a couple of steps right of center most of the time, but I sometimes like to be a step left of center. But I only know that because I've been to both end zones. I grew up eating a la carte. We now live in a world where it's fast food. And value meals. But there are just two value meals: #1 and #2. And if you read that last statement and assigned camps to those numbers, then I'd ask that we recall that teaching about love. Reclaim the spectrum. Visit, with love, the other side.

Looking Up

Judging on a scale of 1 to 10 seems as arbitrary as a scale of 1 to 12. You know. Metric versus English. But you know who impresses me? All those guys that know the millimeter equivalents to sockets in inches. Or the close approximation. The guys who know what socket is a bit big but can be driven over a stripped nut and made to work. I know a guy who can lay under a car on a creeper and stare at the exhaust. And with no measurement, he makes a new one—spatial skills off the charts. Oh, there is a guy I know who built a cabin with a chainsaw. Nothing else, at least for the walls.

It's a wild world of skills needed to get by. Like my mom who never measured a thing when she baked. Pinches. Palmfuls. Handfuls. Splashes. Baking is precise, and she used precise measurements—that were unique to her. They sound not precise. But they were. If we can't see the talent in someone else, then maybe we need to recalibrate our values. Ever see the spiral swirls on a plaster ceiling? Do you know how easy it looks to make them? Do you know how hard it really is?!

I had a church member that baked in a coal stove. There is no thermometer. No way to guess the temperature. There were no instructions like "Bake at 350 degrees for X minutes." Her skill was . . . the best bread I ever ate. If we can't make a habit of looking up at people, then we are probably trying to look down to God. And that's not the right order. May we look up to others—and see the gifts of God.

Between Space

I've hunted hare on the New York/Quebec border a bunch over the years. On a farm owned by a family my wife knows from her childhood. Hare, as you may know, can run a long way. In 2005 or so, I was hunting there over Christmas break. The farmer had said, in the north country accent, "Once you get back in dem der cedars and in da swamp, you'll see so many tracks your dog won't know which way ta go, eh."

And he was right. I hunted all week that we were visiting my in-laws for Christmas. About Thursday, the farmer asked how I was making out. I told him I did really well once I crossed what looked like an old railroad bed. "You walk dat far on da snowshoes?" He asked.

"Yeah."

"You was in Quebec!" He exclaimed. "No big deal before September eleventh!" There were no signs or anything to indicate that I had crossed the border. The next year, I returned. The hare went over two miles and crossed the border. I waited in New York State. It took a long time, but it returned.

There's a term that gets tossed around in philosophy, construction, medicine; you name it. Interstitial space. It means between space. The space between spaces. In parts of Maine, there is a massive clear cut of timber. You know when you hit the Canadian border. It's real clear.

Between spaces are very fluid in the sense of variable or changeable. Think of a border town. Along that Quebec border, you get that French Canadian influence. That culture is on both sides of the border. The border becomes culturally interstitial. Ditto for anyplace on the Mexican border.

Wherever we live, if we are disciples, then we live, or ought to, in the interstitial places of our parish. What do I mean? In good old fashion terms, we live where The Kingdom of God meets the world. The world of faith has a dynamic interaction with the secular world. When we are in Sunday worship, we are in the heart of kingdom space. Not much there that seems secular. Or it shouldn't. But maybe it does? We go out into the world and back. So, in effect, any parish is a border town. Stuff sneaks in. Cultural things. You can see it in fundraisers. Different cultures. You'll see wild game dinners in rural realms. Probably not so much in the burbs. Pork and sauerkraut dinners are common where I live; you won't find that all over the country. Some churches have ham and leek dinners. Wild leeks ain't found everywhere, either! They are a labor-intensive but virtually free food. Dig them. Takes for ever to clean them. Taste like a mixture of garlic and onion. We call them leeks here. In West Virginia, they go by the name ramps.

But it's more than that kind of stuff that crosses the interstitial space. The prosperity gospel, the idea that wealth is what God wants for all of us and is the indicator of good faith and blessing, is an insidious teaching that crosses into our churches from the culture around us that values wealth and "branding" and a life based on pleasures. I'm no proponent of the teaching. It has all the yuckiness of a pyramid scheme and all the heartlessness of one too.

If worship is clearly kingdom space, then what is not? The casino, maybe? Or the bar? Secular values seem to dominate in those places. Here is where I've been driving this whole time about interstitial space: are we more worried that the secular world will swallow us whole, or are we convinced that The Kingdom of God is moving and growing? God's kingdom advances like the tide rolling in. In that sense, I think we ought to be convinced that each one of us inhabits the interstitial space of the Kingdom. It dwells within us. We are the expanding kingdom. We don't retreat from the world that scares us or tempts us, but rather we press forward. We share the Kingdom and bring others in with us. I get random calls from people just to talk about faith. Or Facebook messages. Just because I'm willing to talk about God. I'm not saying I have answers when people are struggling and contact me, but I'm willing to struggle with them. If you're a disciple, you are interstitial space. At local ball games. On the fishing stream. At your place of work. At the Super Bowl party. In your firehall (big thing here in Pennsylvania). At the bowling alley. In the hospital waiting room. In the nursing home. At the funeral home.

In all those places, you will encounter people clearly not in the Kingdom. Not yet believers. Secular. But you are the interstitial space the shows the growing kingdom. You ain't getting overpowered by the evil of this world. You're rolling in to make a difference, and the indwelling spirit moves you across borders. Like the first year I hunted hare and walked into Quebec, not knowing. I just went in and got it done. I'm not advocating that we cross international borders. We have plenty of borders in our own towns. We walk into the world, crossing borders because wherever we go, the Kingdom is found. Sorta borderless, really.

Prophet Punches

Prophecy. Pretty soon, they will take Punxsutawney Phil from his pampered home at the public library to go into a fake stump, and he will then be held high for the world to see. He lives the rest of the year with a gal chuck. Maybe two, I can't remember. But it's a glass sanctuary attached to the public library. College kids party all night on February 1st, and I happen to know that there is good overtime money to be made by state troopers who have to go from all over the state. A church member at our parish was given the option, and his wife told him the overtime rate was too good, so he had to go.

PETA is upset over the live animal. I'll make it worse for them. If you live in central Pennsylvania, you know that Punxsutawney school has the groundhog as a mascot. Wanna guess who their rival is? The DuBois beavers! Both are big tooth, but not fierce, critters. Anyway. When the leaders of the ceremony at Gobbler's Knob hold up the woodchuck and read the weather forecast, they wear top hats. Jeremiah Johnson and all the mountain men were looking for beavers. It takes one large beaver pelt to make one of those traditional top hats. The irony, then, is that as Punxsutawney celebrates the woodchuck, they are wearing the hides of their arch-rival.

Anyway, that's all irrelevant to what I want to discuss. Prophets. Our Christian Old Testament is called the Tanak by our Jewish sisters and brothers. T for Torah. N for Nevi'im. K for Ketuvim. They divide what we call the Old Testament into three parts: Torah (law), Nevi'im (prophets), and Ketuvim (writings). Now, if you watch the TV preachers, you might get the impression that the prophet's whole job was to predict stuff so far in the future that no one living at the time would ever see those predictions. Oh, and that they mostly talked about the end of the world.

Prophecy is not primarily about predicting the future, although there is an element of that at times. Prophet literally means a person who speaks for God. This is what the prophets do. Sometimes dramatically. Isaiah named his first son. Shear-Jashub. He takes the son to see King Ahaz. The story doesn't say that Isaiah told the king the name of his son. But I think he did. "Say hello to king, Shear-Jashub." The boy's name is highly symbolic. It means "A remnant will survive" in Hebrew. Shear is a remnant. It's technical language. War was genocide then. The remnant is the people left after the defeat. The very few not found and killed. The name tells the people what would happen. Then. In that generation. Not a far-off prediction, but one relevant for the time.

By and large, prophets reminded people who they were and how they ought to behave. They denounce greed. Stand up for orphans and widows. Or, like Samuel, they go to the king and tell him that he can't do whatever he wants to do just because he's a king. You can't just sleep with a married woman and have her husband killed. No other country around them had a king that had to follow the law. But in Israel, the king had to follow God's law. A prophet was someone with the bravery to tell the truth to the guy that could have him killed. Prophets didn't punch down. They spoke to the powerful. They didn't go after a bread thief. They went after the corrupt system that would make people so desperate that stealing food was necessary.

Prophets can make us uncomfortable. They remind us that God doesn't ignore the fact that we ignore his standards. Amos told the people that making sacrifices and performing rituals would not save them when they turned around and made a society where almost everyone was in poverty except for a couple of people. He's speaking in his own time.

Bramble Rambles

What do we have to say today? To speak for God? Do we punch down? Throw a jab or a hook at the illegal immigrant working for the big landscaping company? The employer can pay the fine every year and still be money ahead. Way ahead. If the employer gets caught. And if he pays the fine. Employers know if the worker is legally permitted in the country. A local fruit farm employs a lot of legal immigrants. He can't find Americans to do the work. Not for more than a day or two. Not for the pay. An illegal farm pays even less. How much do we value cheap apples? No one wants stiff penalties against the employer. At least no one with power.

Is there a prophet willing to deal with the fact that many senior citizens can't afford their medicine? I know a guy that got billed for a hysterectomy. He kept telling the insurance company he was a man and could not have had that procedure. I know a gal who died, and while on hospice, they gave her every scan and test they could, although she wasn't gonna make it. Why? She was a miner's widow. United Mine Workers insurance pays everything. She was money in the bank. Meanwhile, some people can't get the care that will make a difference because their insurance isn't very good. We tell them to get a better job and better insurance.

A woman is on public assistance. Has a bunch of kids. The kids get their best meal at school. And that ain't saying much. No dad in their lives. Do you blame these kids who have no control over their lives? All this is to say that you will have no trouble finding people who identify problems. Most of them ain't prophets. They punch down while grumbling. Prophets don't do that. It's dangerous work being a prophet. Dietrich Bonhoeffer. Martin Luther King Jr. Bishop Romero. They kill prophets. The people who punch down just make things worse.

Partisans

I find my newsfeed to be a mean place. I think it is perfectly okay to disagree with any politician and use denigrating language even. However, I find it so hard to see terrible blanket statements about all members of the other political party. Two parties and two sides and almost 50/50 in terms of percentages for the nation as a whole. I find that if you leave out the names of politicians and just talk to people, we all want the same things. I'm amazed at how many people completely dismiss half the population. The constant bickering is why I often post a faith-based post dealing with universal topics. The Information Age hasn't produced a lot of wisdom. Information, information everywhere but not a drop of wisdom, to paraphrase Coleridge's *Rime of the Ancient Mariner*.

You can insulate yourself with only people that agree with you. But I'd argue that it's more isolation than insulation. I look at Jesus. He reached out to the other groups. Samaritans. Gentiles. Even when he says negative things (like comparing the Syro-Phoenician woman to a dog), he still helps. Pharisees argued with Jesus, but many of his followers came from their ranks.

When the Sadducees, who did not believe in the afterlife, tried to mock Jesus by proposing a hypothetical scenario where a woman was widowed to seven different men, they wanted to know who she would be married to in the afterlife. Jesus doesn't rant about their position but explains his. So often, we feel that upholding our beliefs must be paired with putting the other person down. It's shocking how the practice of hurting someone else to feel better persists after junior high school.

Jesus healed the child of a Roman centurion. The actual enemy. Way more removed than his fellow Jewish believer of a different position. I do have hope. The meanness often subsides in face-to-face interactions. The anonymity of the keyboard can amplify the anger people have. But in person, there is more restraint. No one is converting anyone to the other side in these political memes and insults. Conversion isn't the specialty of donkeys or elephants. It's a lion thing. The lion from the tribe of Judah, Jesus. He did that by loving people. Even when they were very different from him. I'm not saying people should not belong to a political party. I certainly don't want religious leaders passing laws—some Baptists outlawing dancing, the Methodists stop the lottery, who's gonna lock up divorced people? But in terms of how I interact with people, I choose to follow the Lion, who was also the Lamb of God.

Agony

Reverse circumcision. There. That got your attention. Adult Jewish men did this in antiquity. Tried all sorts of things so that they did not look circumcised. Why? To be athletes. The Greek word for nude is "gymnos." As in gymnasium. Athletics was done in the nude. None of that has anything to do with what I really want to talk about. Agony is the thing. "Agon" means contest. Like wrestling or running or whatever contest would be held. Winners and losers. This is a value that has been enmeshed in our culture. Agonistic endeavors are ritualized and given ceremonial borderline religious significance. The winners are heroes. Exalted. But there must be losers too.

Competition is everywhere. Class rank based on GPA. Making the team. Dating. Those were all while we were still in high school. Getting into the major you want. Getting a job in your field. Getting into a good neighborhood. That gets your kids into a good school district. Repeat it all to emphasize your children's agony (competition). How many TV shows are premised on voting someone off the next episode? Excellence and achievements. Meritocracy. But . . .

Jesus lost. Well, they killed him. He didn't fight back. He made crazy statements like "the last will be first." Blessed are the poor. Turn the other cheek. "Koinonia" is the term for the fellowship or community of faith. It implies that all members are participants. And that rather than voting people out, we do the opposite. Our task is to include. It often doesn't go well.

If you go to any town big enough to have multiple churches of the same denomination, you may discover segregation even within the same faith tradition. Based on money. One church has high-end cars in the parking lot. Another has the Average Joe autos and makes monthly payments. Another has those cars with no monthly payments, needing periodic repairs, and maybe with paint that doesn't match. I've owned a bunch of that kind of vehicle myself. Some were painted with spray cans of Rustoleum by the steady hands of guys with way more skill than I will ever have. Guys that never went to college and can keep any vehicle running.

Koinonia doesn't happen easily because it isn't a value in the culture around us. I went to a very large church in college while getting ready for seminary. They had a lot of students. Close to campus. That's why I went. The non-students who worshipped were diverse, but many were upper-crust. A few thought I was a bit too blue-collar. That's okay; I judged them too. At one meeting, they fought about spending $10,000 on a new stop for the organ. So the organist didn't have to move a bunch of stops between the offertory and the doxology. Depending on the music played during the offertory (music while the collection plates are passed), the pause before the doxology might take ten seconds. They had the money. Thankfully, they voted no.

The big problem with realizing *koinonia* is the whole premise of competition. Do we really think we are better than others? I think we do. Oh, we might use the language "I've been blessed," but it all means that we feel better about ourselves. Smarter or more talented or harder working. I've been the guest at supper with poor people. They want to make sure I got enough. Those meals are like the ones I've always known. People with a bit more means want to ensure the guest likes the taste. For the upper crust, it's theater to feed guests. Entertainment, multiple courses, and more silverware than I know how to figure out. I used to wait and see what fork or spoon to use by watching others around me. I don't care anymore; I just use whatever.

True *koinonia* requires radical egalitarianism that lives the things that we say. Things like are part of the body of Christ. We are one in the Spirit. All are equal under Christ. The smart gal and the guy that struggled to get through high school. The person who will never have much in the bank and those who spend time thinking about $10,000 modifications on the organ.

Now. The real challenge. How do we ensure that we include others rather than voting them off like a reality TV show? Offering a handout and pity to people we view as beneath us won't work. They will go to their own church, one characterized by *koinonia*. Anyway, that's my long answer, or rather a rephrasing of the question, to one of the problems I see in American Christianity. Pastors are just as bad as anyone else when it comes to competition. And as long as we clergy treat the inner city and rural churches as stepping stones to the wealthy, suburbanite, cul de sac churches where pastors would rather be, we are not encouraging *koinonia*.

Gifts

I've been in a lot of Bible studies for a lot of years. One of my favorites is a 32-week curriculum called Disciple. It covers eighty percent of the Bible. Over 32 weeks, the group becomes close. There's a very important event at the end of those 32 weeks . . . Baptism is a radical affirmation of the divine interacting with humans and living as an indwelling presence. If the incarnation is the proclamation of God on earth, then Baptism is the outlandish assertion of God within us. A more profound relationship than the reality that we are all made in God's image. The image is now a vessel of the divine. Of course, this all requires that we take the matter seriously. That we nurture that baptism. That we seek to be disciples.

Anyway, you can find a few laundry lists written by Paul that list the gifts of the spirit. They vary from believer to believer, Christian to Christian, and sister to brother. We focus on those. Sometimes too much. Now, there are fruits of the Spirit that Paul talks about. Love, joy, peace, patience, kindness, goodness, faithfulness, gentleness, and self-control. That list is in Galatians 5. Those things are present in all believers who allow the Spirit to transform us. Every brother and sister displays those nine attributes. So often, debates about gifts lack those nine fruits. It's joyless, mean, and harsh dialogue with no self-control. Those nine are for all of us. If we have trouble feeling gifted, we may see if we bear these nine fruits. If we do not, perhaps we haven't accepted our baptism. Maybe we haven't submitted ourselves to The Spirit. Let's be honest about baptism—it's a spiritual drowning. We die to sin and rise to Christ. We participate in the death and resurrection. What if we decide not to give Christ full reign? Ego and ambition are powerful forces, and the secular world often doesn't value those nine fruits.

But if we bear fruit, then we are living in the spirit. And we are gifted. Romans 12 lists some. 1 Corinthians 12 too. There are other lists. They don't match, so I don't think they are meant to be exhaustive. If we have those nine fruits, we won't be bouncing around with pride. Paul encountered that kind of pride over the baffling gift of tongues that is listed. Whenever someone speaks in tongues, it is always an existing language that the listener knows. Like at Pentecost. The apostles are speaking languages they never studied. Not talking gibberish that no one understands.

No, when people have the fruit, they aren't keen to brag or strut. In fact, I think the opposite can happen—humility will tend to discourage a believer from claiming a gift or gifts from God. That's a problem because the body of Christ only works when we all exercise our gifts. It ain't enough to sit in the pew, sign the attendance pad, and put money on the plate. That's being passive. Like a sponge. Being a sponge is good. Absorb the grace and love of God when we gather. But then leave the sanctuary and be squeezed out. So the divine is taken by you to other places. And used to clean a filthy world. Passive sponges become active agents of cleansing.

That last week of Disciple. One of the things we do, after 32 weeks together, is each person identifies the gifts we see in everyone else. 12-15 people in the group. Imagine 14 other people telling you what your gifts are. It is a powerful moment for everyone. Well, I'm not sure how many are still reading now that we are this many scrolls down the screen. But this is important. If you are reading, please tell at least five believers what gifts you see in them. Call them. Text them. Email. Facebook it. Write a letter and mail it. I love a soaked sponge when I'm cleaning. Don't forget to remind those folks that we need them to use their gifts. Desperately. And be squeezed out to cleanse and heal a broken world.

Comedy

The old formula is misery + time = comedy. The ancients gave us that. I dabble in humor. I write humor in my hunting stories that appear in magazines and my books. I put humor in my weekly homilies at church. They say happy people ain't funny. Humor comes from a dark place. I've been humorous as long as I've been alive. Well, the jokes don't all land. But I don't think I am a sad person. Because there is a difference . . . Now, I'm a country preacher. I walk up to the worst stuff. I've been there for murder. Sudden infant death. Stillbirth. Miscarriage. Cancer. Accidents. Suicide. Sadness abounds.

Clergy walk into sadness. Everyday. Sure, some days we get a marriage or baptism. Or anniversary. But clergy walk into misery every day. And we do that to stand in a shit storm and proclaim Christ's triumph in all places. There's the difference. Those pastors that use humor are not trying to erase pain with time. We are proclaiming victory over death. Right beats wrong. I look at the wrong. And the violence. I stare it down 'cuz Christ is my boss.

Christ tells me to go out. And about. My boss tells me that we all have big work to do. Sharing faith seems small. But it means everything. And even if misery plus time yields comedy, we can be happy again. Humor isn't used in the moment of pain. We find humor somewhere else and let it be a salve. A balm. A dressing. A temporary and brief respite in our lives. And in all tragedy, we say, "This is not the end of the story."

Officiating Sorrow

Darn Facebook memories. It seems like it was nowhere near five years ago, and yet way longer, that I got the phone call asking me to share on here that Andy Purnell had passed in his sleep and that I was to begin preparations for his funeral services. We ran a lot of beagles together. We hunted a lot of rabbits together. We laughed and shared concerns too. Houndsmen showed up out of the woodwork for the services. That funeral home parking lot, the streets, and every nearby parking lot were full of trucks with dog boxes when we held the funeral later. Lion Country Supply closed that day. That doesn't happen to businesses, you know. The whole staff attended the funeral. That had never happened. Andy was a heck of a GPS guru when someone called the store. All those calls got transferred to him. Andy was so good that he'd get to work an hour late every day because he and I were hunting. They didn't fire him.

I have this trick that I do at funerals. When I bury someone I love, and the emotions get to where they might disrupt my speaking, I have a memory on hand. I keep it in the back of my head. It is a memory of some occasion when the deceased made me angry. When I feel grief while speaking—the kind that seems to rise up from the throat like an artesian well of sorrow, I transfer the memory from the back of my mind to the front. And I dwell on it. The whole process lasts a few seconds. It looks like a long pause, which is common in public speaking.

I didn't really have one of those memories for Andy. He was always late when we'd meet to hunt, but it didn't make me mad. He would call me whenever he knew I was driving by the Snappy's gas station in Bald Eagle if he knew I was going to Altoona or Tyrone hospital for work. There's a Subway restaurant in there. He'd then have the most detailed order for a hoagie you could imagine. Somehow he knew every topping. Every sauce or dressing. I'd make him text the orders because they were so specific. It was a real time suck. But I didn't get mad. I just delivered his lunch.

No, sometimes my trick doesn't work. No memory that gets summoned can temporarily shut the spigot on the tears. If that happens, I bite the inside of my cheek a few times. Let the sharp pain refocus my mind and get through a homily. My cheek was still bleeding a bit when we got to the dinner after the funeral, and I put hot coffee in my mouth. But I held it together that day. Somehow. It seems like it was just yesterday and yet way longer than five years too.

I talked to all sorts of people who told me of Andy's secret hunting spot. I knew every spot. I don't think he had secret spots. He just liked hunting with other people, and of all his beagling friends, I lived the closest (distance) to him, I think. Damn Facebook memories. I'm glad I didn't have to bite my cheek to type just now. None of yinz could see me, so I shed a tear or two with a laugh, thinking about those complicated hoagie orders.

Holy Silence

There is that story after the event with the priests of Baal having a showdown with Elijah on Mount Carmel. In 1 Kings 19, Elijah runs for his life. Jezebel wants him dead. In his angst, he seeks God. Elijah is told to step out on Mount Horeb and wait for God. A rock-splitting wind passes. Not God. An earthquake happens. Not God. A fire passes. Not God. Then a still, calm voice. That was God. Sometimes that verse 12 is translated as silence or sheer silence rather than as a still, calm voice. So, is it silence or still calm voice? I don't feel a need to choose, even though the expert translators have to make a choice.

I'm comfortable with a still voice or a silent voice. That's for the word *demamah* in Hebrew. *Demamah* can be still or silent. The other word, *daqqa*, can mean calm or small. Most often, it is used for finely ground. Pulverized, sort of. So really small. I will go with a silent calm voice, combining a few translations. I've never heard God's voice, not audibly. But I've heard God. So a silent voice. But a voice! When we seek a sign from God, I often think a dramatic revelation would be so much easier. A loud, booming voice would work. A powerful wind/earthquake/fire even would help remind me to pay attention. You know, like that friend THAT SENDS YOU TEXTS IN ALL CAPITAL LETTERS. It gets annoying when your friend does that every time. But if God would be so good as to make it all really clear in capital letters, I would be glad. But He doesn't. It's a silent voice.

I'm good at being quiet. I sometimes have to function as an extrovert, but I'm naturally an introvert. In seminary, I had my favorite prof four semesters in a row. I turned in an assignment early for the course in that fourth semester and explained that I was serving a parish and had to miss class to officiate a funeral on the day the assignment was due. He asked me what class it was. He didn't know I was in there. I was that silent. I always sat in the back. Never talked. In any class. Unless I needed a question answered.

Being quiet, however, is only part of it. As good as I am at that, there is also the need to listen for the silent voice. Wind, fire, and earthquakes may not abound, but I can provide my own noise, even while not making sound myself. Satellite radio, Pandora, and songs on my iPhone probably provide the most noise in my life. I love music. Television can also rattle. I've never been much of a video game guy, but I have that darned Words With Friends on my phone.

There's a lot of noise. I once tried to listen to a person in a hospital waiting room, and there were many other, louder conversations going on amongst other people in the room. Likewise, the TV was blaring some talk show with a whole bunch of people (I guess they call that a panel) talking at once, forming a cacophony rather than a dialogue. I missed the very audible voice next to me. Couldn't hear it. Then I wonder how easy it must be to drown out an inaudible voice, a silent voice. Add email, texts, and social media, and we can have multiple layers of noise that we choose (some of it also silent to our ears), making it hard to hear God's calm, silent voice.

Learning to listen anew. To a voice that is profound, real, and silent. Oh, and when God talks to Elijah, the prophet is told to seek out other believers. We are called to devotional time with God and corporate time with God and other believers—worship and fellowship. When we listen for the silent voice, we must ensure we don't mistakenly hear ourselves. Sometimes turning off the music, TV, and computer isn't enough; we have to turn down our racing thoughts to let God speak. You will never hear if you use a CB or a walkie-talkie, and never let go of the button that lets you speak. But we can hear if we listen and let go of the talk button. Silence can be oppressive for some. Solitude is unbearable for them. But if we seek it and practice, we can learn to be alone for important listening time. Learn to be comfortable in our own minds. And ultimately, able to quiet our thoughts to be open to listening to that silent and calm voice. When prayer moves from holding the talk button to letting go of the button and finding the divine in the silence. No need to seek big signs when we have access to the holy in silence.

Status

One time, my wife wrote a resume for me, and when I read it, I could not help but be impressed with me. Granted, it was a resume version of me, not really me. It was, at the very least biased, with the best foot forward and hide the faults attitude. Then, of course, you have those interview questions. They happen when you are looking for a job to get you to admit your faults, and we provide creative answers to get around showing our shortcomings.

"What are your weaknesses?"

"Oh, you know, I work too many hours, and everyone says I have too much energy. My attention to detail is borderline aggravating. People get jealous that I catch all the tiny mistakes before something bad happens."

I was once in an interview for a job I didn't necessarily want. I was asked, "So, why are you the best person for the job?"

"I don't know that I am," I said, "I did not meet the other applicants." I got the job, which was shocking. Resumes are always in plain view. When you meet someone new, one of the first questions you will be asked is, "What do you do for a living?" You'll be judged on the answers. We assign value to people based on their occupation. More than that, we assign a financial value based on your answer. You are worth X dollars per hour. And someone else is worth Y dollars per hour. or maybe Z thousand dollars per year if it is an annual salary.

In Paul's letter to the Philippians, he throws his resume out in chapter 3. It is directed at people who have, it seems, offered their resumes to new believers and perhaps were being exclusive. He says that he himself was circumcised on the 8th day. In other words, he was born Jewish. Perhaps he was arguing with a convert, a gentile who converted later in life. Converts can be zealous and feel like they are really getting it right. Maybe it was a God-fearer he was arguing against. These gentiles never fully converted to Judaism but were attracted to the core teaching. Why did they not fully convert? Adult circumcision without anesthesia would have been required for full conversion. They followed all the rules except that one. Paul continues, listing that he is from the tribe of Benjamin. So maybe he is arguing with a fellow Jewish believer and stating his status. Paul then says that he was a Pharisee (really followed the law) and so on.

Then, he counts it all as loss; none of it matters compared to gaining Christ. Now, perhaps you have friends that cuss a lot. "That blankity blinking filth foul blasted blanker!" Maybe you are the friend that uses a lot of cuss words. I once had someone apologize to me for cussing since I am a pastor. The person obviously did not know that my father was a colossal cusser, a true vendor of vulgarity. I replied, "The only words that bother me are the ones that I cannot define. So far, we are good; no need to apologize." My dad could use the F-bomb as a preposition. That ain't easy.

But when you use cuss words constantly, they lose their power. They are just like articles such as "the" or a piece of punctuation. They are just generic adjectives if you cuss frequently. In Philippians 3:8, Paul drops a cuss word. The S-word. The bad word we don't want our kids to say, so we teach them "going #2." He doesn't say bowel movement, poo, or crap. He uses the bar room Greek cuss word. It usually gets translated as rubbish, filth, or something much more sanitized. But it stands out because Paul doesn't write those words. You really notice the vulgarity and that he equates it to his achievements and privilege. In effect, he is saying that everything we use to compare ourselves to each other is useless. We

Bramble Rambles

don't find our value in dollars per hour, an office instead of a cubicle, or a luxury car over an old beater. Our value is found completely in the fact that we all belong to Christ. The rest, Paul says, is *skubala*. It's an S-word in Greek too.

Thoughts on Scripture

The parameters of the ways we can view scripture have two opposite poles. One is that these are simply stories written by religious people about their god, and they are no more representative of the divine than stories written by the Greeks, the Egyptians, the Norse, or the Maya. The other pole, one of literalism, is that these books that comprise the Bible are words piped directly from God and written verbatim by a human author, but one possessed by the holy to make the person a conduit only, and the author is God. Most Christians are in between, though we can be closer to one pole than the other. Some groups incorporate philosophy, science, and tradition into faith. Others rely on the Bible alone.

One thing is certain, what we claim the Bible says has more impact than what it does say. Interpretations vary, and some people interpret better than others. To that end, a verse must be read within a chapter, and that chapter within the book and that book within the entire scope of the Bible. Some awful things exist in the Bible. Just Genesis alone has murder, incest, slavery, prostitution, theft, a guy banishing a woman he got pregnant along with their kid into the desert, a revenge plot that involves making adult males accept circumcision and then killing them while they are too injured to fight, and a guy sending his wife to have sex with another guy.

Bob Ford

You can justify almost any horrible thing with the Bible. Race-based slavery fully emerged as an interpretation of that story in Genesis 9, where Ham's son Canaan is cursed to slavery—and some terrible analysis of the test led many to say that Ham's descendants were Africans. That was an interpretation with lasting and reverberating repercussions. In other words, interpretation is where the faith gets real. Some preachers are better than others. Good writers (theology or sermons) are good readers. It's worth noting that devout readers of scripture also led the way in ending legal slavery. Good readers.

Regarding those two poles, I will say that the Bible is our primary source of revelation, but the church is older than scripture. Nobody was writing this stuff down as it happened. Living in their time, people of faith wrote about their experiences as people of faith. The writing, however, happened after reflection, not in real-time like modern reporting on cable news.

So, the tough part is determining what parts of scripture are prescriptive for all time and what parts are descriptive of the time when those words were written. Things like slavery and warfare that occurred in a world where genocide was the cultural norm, polygamy, and other practices described the time when they occurred. Covenant, discipleship, transformative grace, speaking truth to powerful people, and other themes are certainly prescriptive for all times.

Early on, the church proclaimed that Jesus was fully divine and fully human. We can see that. The divinity in his birth, miracles, resurrection, and Ascension. There's also the humanity. He gets tired. At one point, he doesn't seem to know when figs are in season, he gets tempted, and he has no idea when he is coming back, though he knows that he will. Hunger. Sorrow. All the very human stuff applies to Jesus Christ, the incarnate word of God.

And the Bible, in my thinking, is also fully divine and fully human and hand copied for centuries before the printing press. The big brains (fundamentalists and liberals alike) study the tiny differences in those manuscripts that survive from thousands of years ago. Therefore, when I read the fully divine word, I don't get hung up on the fact that Genesis has two different creation stories right next to each other, or that no two gospels have the same list of the 12 apostles, or the oddity wherein The Gospel of John has Jesus crucified on a different day than Matthew, Mark, & Luke have all agreed was Friday. John has to have Jesus crucified a day earlier (Passover) because, for him, Jesus is the new Passover lamb.

When people have an experience of God, they communicate the event the best they can, and while God inspires, you can't fully describe an experience. No matter how much you read, you didn't know what it would feel like to ride a horse, get pneumonia, eat apple pie, have your first kiss, or be a parent. I can only accurately describe the smell of a carnival to someone who has been to one. Biblical authors describe some things we have experienced and some that we haven't. The Bible is the foundation of faith. Some people interpret it better than others. And those interpretations have serious ramifications.

Evil

Augustine spoke of evil as the absence of good. In other words, evil was actually the nonexperience of goodness. It is the privation of good. In other words, he said that evil wasn't real, but rather what we experience as evil is the absence of goodness. It is sort of like the reality of cold being the absence of heat. There is the coldest temperature in the universe. It is -459.67 degrees Fahrenheit or 0 degrees on the Kelvin scale. Cold is merely the absence of heat. Being deprived. In my head, I like the idea of evil being that lack of goodness. But in my heart, it doesn't sit well, like your dentist telling you that you do not have a cavity but an absence of enamel. Or the highway department tells you that there are no potholes. There is simply a lack of asphalt. No, I think evil exists, and you and I have experienced it.

The only *easy* way to explain evil is to say that one of the three things we say about God is false. We say God is 1. Omniscient (all-knowing) 2. Omnipotent (all powerful) & 3. Omnibenevolent (All good). We can easily explain evil events if we say that God either didn't know about it or couldn't stop it. Or scarier yet, say that God isn't all good. But we maintain that God is all of the above. Monotheism is difficult. In ancient cultures with many gods, the good gods ran the show when good things happened. The bad gods were in control in difficult times.

Bob Ford

You have no easy answers when you live between the monotheistic parameters of omniscience, omnipotence, and all goodness. But you can have all the questions you want. And this is where we must leave the head and enter the heart and a life of prayer. I ask questions. I argue. I even yell a little. The same as I do with people that I love. If I can do that with my fellow humans, I certainly can with God. Never yelled at God? You can. Never disagreed with God? It's a good thing to do. We yell and argue with the people closest to us. Polite and civil conversations always take place in the public sphere. In some ways, if we cannot argue with God, then we aren't that close.

Here are some more divine traits that have their origins not in the Bible but in Greek philosophy and metaphysics: 1. Immutability (never changing) and 2. Invulnerability. A proper god had to be invulnerable, not to be hurt and unchanging, because if the god changed, it must have been imperfect before the change. None of this is biblical, but as Christianity moved out of biblical lands, it acquired aspects of the surrounding culture, and Greek thinking was added, often for the benefit of spreading the gospel.

People smarter than I have argued that if you are invulnerable, then you cannot love. When we love someone, we are subject to being hurt by them. A harsh word from a loved one is painful. At the heart of it all, we affirm that God loves us, and he loves us perfectly. This perfect love, perhaps, demands vulnerability and change to be in a relationship with people who are very vulnerable and constantly changing as we go through life. God abides through the worst of it all. God can change his mind. Did it in the Bible all the time. Prayer is the vehicle that puts us in dialogue with a God vulnerable enough to love unconditionally and changing enough to save us. Indeed, prayer is an affirmation that change is always a possibility. God's love is meant to transform (change) believers and the world we live in.

I still like Augustine's intellectual assertion that evil is simply the absence of good. But when suffering strikes, it makes for a less-than-satisfactory response. Love, on the other hand, is always a fitting response in the face of suffering, and while it does not answer how a tragedy happened or why, it offers a way forward. When someone asks, "Why me?" after a terminal diagnosis from a physician, it does not answer that question. It does, however, affirm that in all circumstances where we might ask "why me?" we will be sure to find a God that goes with us, a god who willingly suffers and dies. And rose again, offering us the same destiny. He broke the trail for us on that first Easter, a trail leading out of death and into eternity. And he not only made the trail, but he will also be our trail guide when our time comes.

Hesed

We routinely learn a little bit of a foreign language to feed our bellies. Cacciatore, paella, spanakopita, bratwurst, and coq au vin are all words that get used with some regularity that are imported into English. We could do the same with a few Hebrew and Greek words without too much effort if our hunger were the same. The Hebrew word *Hesed* would be a great dish to start with.

It is all over the Psalms (as well as other parts of the Old Testament) and was traditionally translated as "lovingkindness." It is that grace and love that is extended that can never be repaid, and we understand that. Like all the good things that parents give their kids. Kids don't repay lovingkindness. I mean, they may very well return loving-kindness when they are older, but not as infants. And not in a way that could be construed as paying off a love debt of some kind.

God extends lovingkindness to humanity. People seem more reluctant to extend such *hesed* to others unless it is a relative or good friend. In fact, the word is translated as lovingkindness when describing God's love for his people. *Hesed* tends to translate as mercy or kindness when describing interactions among people. But it is all *hesed*. Understanding *hesed* is essential if we can make sense of what Paul is talking about whenever he discusses mercy. *Hesed* becomes *maga eleos* in Greek—great mercy.

Hesed is rooted in zeal and passion. It is not a legalistic term. That being said, the Greek *eleos* is often associated with the pagan goddess Clementia. The word where we get clemency, which is a legal term today. No, whatever else *hesed* is, it is passionate and zealous love from God. God is as much our advocate as our judge in that sense. This is the great joy of faith—our judge is our advocate. A passionate advocate who loves us.

If we want to translate *hesed* as lovingkindness all the time—interactions between humans and divine relationships with humans, then we simply must have the source of *hesed* be divine. If you are to extend divine love, then it must be generated from God. In that sense, we are called to be conduits of *hesed*. That is how we love the unlovable. Because God loved us when we were unlovable, and he does so again through us.

Cross Over Karma

I know it is popular to invoke karma to rejoice when something bad happens to someone who did something bad. The roots of karma are millennia old and date back to the caste system in Hindu society. I'm certainly no expert in eastern religions, and I'm not writing to disparage the Hindu religion. But the caste system allowed for institutional segregation of the classes that sent all benefits to the upper classes and relegated the lower castes to a very difficult life. Especially a fifth group so low it did not even make the caste system—the untouchables. They were so low you did not touch them. The poorest of the poor. I know we also have problems in the West with abject poverty and can voluntarily not associate with the poor. But we know it is not the will of Christ. He chooses the poor. The bottom of the barrel is his gang. He operated at the underbelly of society to change things and ordered us to do the same.

Karma is rooted in a belief in reincarnation. If you behave well in this life, you will return to a higher caste in the next life. If you behave immorally, you come back to a lower caste. No one changed social status in life; you had to wait for death and reincarnation. Behave long enough, attain a virtuous life, and you can escape the endless cycle altogether, a state of bliss called *moksa*. Each one of your reincarnated lives maintains a ledger sheet, and the goal is to climb through the castes and escape the misery of life. I am oversimplifying the doctrine, but that is the gist of it. It was developed to help explain the reality of suffering.

Not only does the Christian tradition not utilize a belief in reincarnation, but it also has a deep taproot that shows a divine favor for the downtrodden, powerless, and poor. This is true even though many Christians have not been faithful to the calling that we have been given. I've often said that working with the poor is scary. What if poverty is "catchy," as in contagious? It's probably worse than contagious, actually. It's a perpetual possibility. How many paychecks can any of us miss? One? None? Medical bankruptcy is a reality for many people. I know a guy that lives in his vehicle because of medical bills, which caused him to sell his house. The popular usage of karma as a leveling of the moral scales in this lifetime is not true. Good people have it bad sometimes. People who act cruelly often thrive. As Christ tells us in The Sermon on the Mount, the sun rises on the evil and the good, and life-giving rain falls on the just and unjust.

Karma is rooted in free will. Your free will determines your morality and your destiny in the next life. Free will lies at the heart of Christian ethics too. We are agents of our own actions. And we all have immoral moments. Sin. Aren't you glad you don't receive karmic repercussions for all those things? All the things we do and think? That's the cross in Christianity. Christ received all punishment. The book of Hebrews is more specific. Christ was not only the sacrifice for sin; He is the high priest that made the sacrifice. He was the priest and lamb. A self-offering, not a victim.

I don't think we use the word karma in pop culture as it is meant in the Hindu faith. In so many ways, it's worse. It's a hope and desire to see bad things happen to people who have hurt us or don't like us. By contrast, Christ said, "Forgive them, for they know not what they do." He said this about the people that tortured him. Scourged him. Nailed him to a piece of wood. When I think of that, it makes me feel horrible for being so petty that I might feel genuine disgust for someone that inconveniences me in some small way—like taking 30 items through the express lane at the store.

Grace is the deliberate application of God's love to the brokenness of this world. It's not the punting of a moral balance to the hope that we will be born again with a hope for a better life. Grace is the realization that we are born again in this current life through the Holy Spirit, and therefore we will die only once—to rise again with Christ, never needing to be reincarnated. We don't start again like resetting a video game. No matter how many attempts we would get, we can never be sinless or blameless. Instead, we are saved in this one life we get. The YOLO of pop culture. We are transformed by grace, restored, and made to be agents of change, liberation, and hope in this world.

Bob Ford

Living

The myth of Sisyphus is basically a guy condemned to roll a huge rock up a hill all day, only to watch it roll down. So, he does it again, and it rolls down. Again. This is his day, every day. I've often said that if our lives are to wake up and go to work to pay the bills to go to bed and go to work and pay the bills—well, we are no different. We just have a different rock and a different hill.

Being a spectator contributes to this *Groundhog Day* lifestyle. If life is about the local sports teams and recording TV shows, we aren't living. We are watching. A Yanomami woman moved from the Amazon (jungle, not the business) to America and eventually returned. She said that Americans live in boxes (houses) and watch other people actually live on other boxes (television, pre-flat screen). Might be spot on.

I'm moved by people who are not spectators. People who are doing things. I try to do things. What a life if we go to our graves with statistics of athletes memorized and massive chunks of multiple movies memorized, and we've done nothing else. Just watched other people live. Real people or fictitious! If you choose to push the rock, it is hard to live. The rock is so miserable it's great to spectate a better life. This is more true because, as a culture (all cultures), we define you by your rock. In other words, what do you do for a living? It's almost always one of the first questions we ask people.

You can be defined and reduced to dollars per hour. What is your job, and how much status does it bestow? Life ought to be more. Your family. Your passions. Your hobbies. Your God.

God lifts us up and lets us be living participants in a great kingdom. Read that analogy of the body that Paul talks about in 1 Cor 12. There is no greater or lesser task. It's all about working together. We may live vicariously through sports and literature, but the only real vicarious participation is in that trip from the cross to the empty tomb. We do participate in eternity because of Christ. Don't get stuck on today or tomorrow if you belong to eternity. If you belong to eternity, you shouldn't be a slave to yesterday and all the regrets and mistakes. If you belong to eternity, evaluating people based on their jobs would be beneath you. You can see more than that.

Translation

The King James Bible was authorized by King James and completed in 1611. A half-century earlier, in 1540, the Geneva Bible was made. In Geneva, of course. Many English Protestants had fled there during the reign of Queen Mary. The Geneva Bible was a popular English translation. Like many bibles today, it had commentary to help the reader. It was the first to do that in English. Much of that commentary was rooted in Calvinism and supported a more free church. Free from the control of The Church of England.

The commentary and translation irked King James. He felt that it was anti-clergy and anti-monarch. Being a monarch himself, James was bothered by this. So, he authorized a new translation. It's called The Authorized Translation, but we now commonly call it King James, over 400 years later. It was intentionally pro-King and pro-church hierarchy.

The Pilgrims and many other colonists arrived in America with the Geneva Bible. Colonists were anti-King, as we know. We call those Plymouth Rock arrivals Puritans, but they were separatists. Puritans wanted to purify The Church of England. Separatists felt it was too late for that, so they separated. The gang going to Plymouth had fled to Holland because they worshipped on their own. Not in The Church of England. That was illegal. They were the folks in the *Mayflower*. Guess what Bible they used? Geneva.

The Authorized Version meant that some other bible was not authorized. Specifically the Geneva Bible. James forbade the use of the word Tyrant in his translation. When his authorized version did not enjoy good sales while competing with The Geneva Bible, he forbade any other translation from being printed. No New Geneva Bibles could be legally printed.

But they kept printing them. And they put the date 1599 on them, even though they were printed in the 1600s. In America, English Bibles were imported from England. That meant King James. Interestingly, there were King James Bibles with Geneva commentary!

Translators make choices all the time. Let's not pretend that they don't. If you get a parallel Bible, it will have several translations side by side. A Jewish poet said that reading the Bible in a translation is like kissing your bride through the veil.

Most of us require a translation. I play with the original languages but haven't kept up the rigorous work I did in seminary. You can teach yourself Greek and Hebrew. And even a little effort can help make a difference and show the text in a new and inspiring way.

The translation is itself an interpretation. Interpreters vary, and some are better than others. Here's where I have been headed the whole time: Idolatry is forbidden. We should not have idols. You would be hard-pressed to find someone who takes Scripture more seriously than I do. But when I see a verse removed from its chapter and book and the whole Bible, it is often used to justify something that the verse never intended to say. And this is done because of our high regard for the Word of God. But, it is possible to turn the Bible itself into an idol. "Bibliolatry."

Read many bibles. Many translations. Study some ancient languages. When we see those differences, we see the dynamism of the Word. Its power. Its purpose. Then it's The Living Word of God, not just words on a page.

Martha and Mary

At the end of Luke's 10th chapter is that story about the sisters Mary & Martha receiving Jesus and the apostles into their home. I like to think this is the same Mary & Martha with the brother Lazarus, but who knows? The text doesn't say for sure. Lots of ink gets used in that debate.

Martha takes care of all the hard work of receiving guests and offering food. You know how your grandma piled food on the table for you as a kid? That was a cultural norm in ancient Judea. Even for strangers. It could be life and death, especially where water is concerned. Mary listens to Jesus. This was a time that had very defined gender roles, and Martha was upset that Mary was not helping with the provisions. She listened to Jesus. Moreover, when Martha complained to Jesus about this, Jesus explained that Mary had chosen the better thing and it would not be taken. Lots of ink has been used on this story to see it as a text legitimizing women in ministry. There's no doubt that women have always been vital to the life of the church. My wife is clergy. I don't need to be convinced about this issue. And I think the main issue is something else.

The life of kids is scheduled now. They have play dates. Parents actually schedule play. That's when they aren't at organized athletics or extracurricular activities. So, they have organized free time. When I was a kid, we woke up in the summer, did what we knew we had to do in terms of chores, and then ran out the door. Staying home meant more chores. If you said you were bored, you might have to split a cord of wood. We were gone all morning and all day. We played baseball, caught crayfish, rode bicycles, read comic books, traded baseball cards, went fishing, walked in the woods, built tree forts that make most of my adult deer hunting stands look pretty paltry, and otherwise did whatever. No one cared where we were. You had to be home at suppertime.

At dinner/lunch/whatever your cultural origins call the noontime meal, there was no way to predict where the barbarian horde of us kids would show up to eat. Our mothers kept jars upon jars of peanut butter and jars upon jars of jelly. Loaves of bread were kept on hand. No one knew where we were. They all had to be prepared when we got hungry, and a gang of kids showed up.

You could tell when we arrived at a house lacking bread. The mom would start quivering and get nervous. She would quickly call someone to make a bread run.

After the sandwiches, moms kicked us to the curb. This was done with generic brand freeze pops or popsicles. Usually, the pops. Remember those? They were in plastic tubes so thick you all but needed a hacksaw to cut through them. They didn't even have a flavor listed. You just called them by their color. I liked blue.

That stuff was messy, so moms kicked us out to eat them. Our faces and shirts were stained red, blue, purple, whatever. Crisis averted. The kids ate and left.

I suspect it was a lot like that when the Jesus Road Show arrived. Chaos. All those followers. Just the 12 would be overwhelming. What if others hung on the outskirts? These are wandering homeless people.

Today, we go to cookouts or dinner parties, and people get creative. We outdo one another on the dishes. Or the appetizers. Or whatever. Jesus ministered to people that were living hand to mouth. Each day was a struggle.

I read the story now and wonder how Martha could have been upset. Jesus was in her house. How could you fault Mary for wanting to listen to Jesus? Are you kidding me? Lord and savior in your house, and you're worried about the details of the visit? Of course, I'm separated by almost 2,000 years from the event. And a huge cultural shift away too.

No, Jesus tells Mary she was worried and upset by many things. But there was only one thing needed. Mary was doing that one thing. Listening at Jesus's feet.

I was visiting a monastery once, and there was a quote that read, "Don't just do something; sit there." It makes me think of Mary, sitting there at Jesus' feet while Martha was doing something. Many somethings, actually.

It takes great practice to sit at Jesus's feet today. We don't hear an audible voice. We are connected through the indwelling Holy Spirit to Christ.

Just sitting there, it seems, is dreadfully rare. It's hard to be alone with our own thoughts. Let alone clear those thoughts to make room for God. You can avoid it altogether. TV. Radio. Internet. You can have constant background noise. Know any elderly people that keep the television on all day just for background noise?

I've always said that good deer hunters can learn to be with Christ. At least they can be alone with their thoughts. Sit. For hours. And hours. Many people can't.

Heck, the kids we hunt with can only sit for a remotely long time on a deer stand if they are at the top of a hill where the cell phone works. They can text. Surf the web.

Being alone with our own thoughts is hard today. The next step is to put self away and make room for God. I can focus on prayer, and then I get distracted. I remember something I did. I recall a task I need to do. I'm back to self. Not God.

So, I sometimes find it helpful to replace my many human words with the Word of God. I use a technique that I often use when working on a sermon. I read a Bible when I'm trying to spend time with Jesus. I read from the Gospels. Right away, I've replaced my words with the Word. I pick a Gospel story. Then, I ask myself: 1. What does this text say about people? 2. What does it say about God? 3. What does it say about the interaction of people with God? Now I am listening to Jesus. Doing the one thing that is necessary.

We live in a world with so much bread that people avoid it. To lose weight. When I was a kid, some moms would abandon the peanut butter and jelly. They might try to make pizza. Or burgers. Or hotdogs. A bit of maternal competition. We really didn't care. We just wanted to eat and get back to being kids. Most moms quickly realized that peanut butter and jelly was good enough. Maybe Martha put too much into the role of hostess. The text says she was distracted. Focus is key. Don't just do something. Sit there. At Jesus's feet. Like Mary.

Beagles are rolling a rabbit in a cornfield. Morning dew is a great scent. I can't see them. But the music is helping me focus. Rabbit ain't coming out. I will have to wander in that corn to catch them when I'm done.

Camping

In the prologue of John, there is that statement that the word became flesh and dwelt (*eskenosen* in Greek) among us. It means to pitch your tent. Camping. The $64 words that get bantered about all the time are transcendence and immanence.

Transcendence means that God is beyond us. Indeed, the original use of Holy (*Kadosh* in Hebrew) meant less a moral distinction and more an ontological one or a different being. Holy is not like us. Incidentally, the three-time use of *kadosh kadosh kadosh* (think Isaiah's vision) is intended to be holiest. Three tunes were the superlative, as opposed to the comparative, for you grammar fans. So when we sing "Holy, Holy, Holy . . ." we are saying holiest. Superlatively Holy.

Anyway, the transcendence of God is divinity 101. But many religious systems could have a transcendent god, including deism which says that God made the laws of physics, created the world, put it in motion, and left it alone. The great watchmaker.

John emphasized immanence in this cosmic camping trip, where the word takes on flesh and pitches a tent. And any Greek-speaking Jew of the day would recognize that the same word was used in the Torah to describe the Tabernacle where God resided, with limited access by humans, until the Temple was built.

God went camping and interacted with everybody from lepers and tax collectors to Pilate, the executioner, and the religious leaders who had the most to lose if this tent was going to somehow make the monumental architecture of Herod's Temple null and void.

Immanence is God inserting himself right into the nonholy. The mundane. The ordinary. I like the picture by Rembrandt, the one of the calming of the sea. The painting is before it is calmed. If you count, there are 13 apostles on that boat. Rembrandt was famous for putting a self-portrait in his paintings. He's holding the rope of the sail. Google it.

That dwelling among us, by the word, is imminence. Incarnational imminence that allows God to be both above it all and in the thick of it. Above it all is important. Big picture. In the thick of it is radical.

The tent/tabernacle was replaced by Solomon's Temple and then Herod's. When Christ died on the cross, Matthew says that the veil within the Temple was ripped when Jesus died. This visually represents the democratization of the Spirit—which went to a select few in the Old Testament—and allows it to be available to all believers now. That's very radical. And forces me to wonder how it is that the nicest people I know are all Christians. Oh, and so are the meanest people I know. That'll have to be left for some other coffee ramble on ecclesiology. Another day. It's all iced coffee today, BTW.

Different Kind of Radical

Early Christians proclaimed Jesus as divine. This would be in direct conflict with another. The Roman emperor was also identified as a god on earth. The kingdom of God was in direct conflict with the empire of Rome. That spiritual kingdom baffles Pilate in the gospel accounts as he tries to determine what kind of King our messiah really is.

Make no mistake, Jesus was killed for being an insurgent against the empire. A spiritual insurgent. Crucifixion was how you were executed for a capital crime if you were a non-citizen. If you were a citizen, you got a quick death via decapitation. Jesus was not crucified between two thieves. They had to be far more dangerous for that death penalty. Not common thieves. That isn't a capital crime. Those two had to be more dangerous to Rome than a common thief. And only Rome could execute. The priests and others may have had a problem with Jesus. A few may have wanted him dead. But only Rome could give that order. For being treasonous against Rome.

The Sicarii (murderers) were a radical group of Jewish zealots. They killed people. Often fellow countrymen that were known collaborators with Rome. They killed the people that did Rome's dirty work. Rome didn't replace governments as they conquered people. They just made the local governments do their bidding.

Ever think about why Jesus had followers named "Sons of Thunder?" Ever wonder why Peter had a sword to cut off an ear in the Garden of Gethsemane? Doesn't Iscariot sound a lot like Sicarii?

Jesus, I think, attracted radicals. And he transformed their zeal from attacking the earthly empire with swords to serving a spiritual kingdom that totally subverted Rome. Eventually. Perhaps it's possible that Judas Iscariot betrayed Christ to force the hand of Jesus. Maybe he felt that when Pilate had Jesus, the messiah would start acting like a messiah. He would kill the bad guys. Eject Rome. Restore the throne of David, get rid of the traitor Herod, and take his crown as a rightful heir of David.

Barabbas is the freed prisoner. A murderer. A freedom fighter. The crowd chose him over the seemingly impotent Jesus. Interestingly, Barabbas means son of the father in Aramaic. As in the Heavenly Father. And there is the choice. The spiritually subversive Christ. And the violence of Barabbas.

One offers salvation through his own redemptive death. The other offers what seems to be salvation through redemptive violence against the enemy.

We blame that crowd. Today. In 21st-century America. How could they not choose Christ? The false promise of redemptive violence seems good for the oppressed. When people are starving and taxed into oblivion. Rome auctioned the right to tax a region. Like, say, Judea. The highest bidder paid Rome immediately. That bidder then got to tax the people. And had to make more than was just given to the empire. To do this, they got local thugs. Like Matthew. And the other tax collectors that Jesus ate with.

I could see myself choosing Barabbas. I could see Jesus as weak if I were living under imperial oppression and in the shadow of the barracks of the Roman Army.

The salvific sacrifice of Christ is the solution. But it doesn't look better than the redemptive violence of Barabbas. I'm not sure we would make the right choice today. Then again, the choice was never ours. It was God's choice. The enemy was more than Rome. It is sin and death.

Bramble Rambles

Rome just happened to deal out both quite well. But they didn't have a total monopoly on sin and death. And Christ defeated both. Crucifixions weren't uncommon. Most had no idea the world had changed. Just another dead radical.

Beyond Objects

Prayer is an activity that is hard to define. It can be very verbal for me, wherein words are in a stream, whether spoken or simply scrolling through my head. It can also be more meditative in an attempt to silence all those words that are pretty much always in my head. A time to give up how we spend most of our day: As the subject of our own little world. I'm talking about subject in the grammatical sense. "I" is a subject. I am the subject of my life. I do things, and as I do things, I interact with other people and things. Those people and things are objects in the world that are focused on I. To that end, I objectify everything. Breakfast. The books I read. The music I play. Even people. The person ringing up my coffee is objectified as a source of caffeine, and the guy who cuts me off in traffic is objectified as an obstacle. I might even dehumanize that driver. And only think of him as his vehicle. He is no longer Joe on a commute to work, stuck in his own "I" world where he sees everyone and everything as objects. He's just a damned silver Honda CRV.

So, now we are spinning on an earthly axis while making solar circuits around the sun with billions of people all seeing the same world as a stage where (s)he is the subject and everyone else and everything else, are merely subjects in the great drama club play of "I." The countless other billions of people are simply the supporting cast.

Each person lives this way. Billions of individual "I" plays/movies are concurrently being lived at once where everyone is the star (self) while simultaneously seeing everybody else as the non-star (The Other). The Other, in the philosophical sense, is different and not the Self. Them. Yuck.

The problem of self and ego. It goes beyond the CRV in traffic and extends to competition for jobs, status, money, a mate, and children. These things, too, are objectified. The job becomes the career that is the objectified pathway to an improved life. The advertising world has no shortage of money being objectified as the concrete evaluator of jobs. You are a better person with more status if you have more. Prospective mates are certainly objectified in a world where we think modern times have hypersexualized everything, but in truth, we probably don't objectify people any more than we ever did since the beginning of time. We just have television commercials to make it mainstream, as sex is used to sell everything and anything. More objects. Even our kids can become objects. We can try to live our lives through them or make them be just like us, even if they are not. It's a world that values athletics and academics, and the objectifying process devalues the kid who runs a slow mile and is a C student. Or so the selfish way of objectifying everyone and everything would have us believe.

So, prayer, for me, is a lot about making it all less me. Less I. And more Other. If I can clear my mind of all words, then the nouns and pronouns are gone, with all the other words. No subject, direct object, and indirect object. Remember sentence diagrams from high school?

Meditative prayer can take a person to a world without subject or objects. Though, I would argue, it is actually moving us to the realm where the Subject is God. Once the grammar of life is gone, we are free to enter the divine. And let's face it—the subject & object worldview is primarily about power. Get rid of the grammar of power, and we see that God is the source of power.

Now, as contemplative prayer silences the words, the true power of God can be experienced. Awareness of interdependence. The buzzing bee pollinates future meals. The birds overhead spread seeds of future berries. Somebody not yet born will have a profound impact on your future great-great-great-grandchildren. Maybe someone with a connection to the damned silver CRV.

And perhaps the CRV isn't just a car. It is a metaphor for The Other. The people I don't like. For whatever reason. Interconnection as we try to see how God must see this world. And the billions of people on it. As God must look upon our silly grammar of power that is implicit in the I lifestyle.

Now we are really playing games to think we can don the lenses of the holy. Pretend we can see the world as God does. That's a crazy idea that I'm proposing at the outset. But since we are talking about prayer, maybe we can see a bit of what it means to void our thoughts of the grammar that embodies subjects and objects laced with struggles for power. We can see it a bit in the way we were taught to pray. "Our Father . . ."

Ooh. Not an I. An our. We. Perhaps the closest we can get to breaking the grammar of power is acknowledging that we were never taught to pray alone. Even when we pray while physically distant from other believers. Alone in our house.

Oooh. What if prayer can take my focus from The Other (a negative concept) and shift it to other believers? Go through that Lord's Prayer. It's all plural. Our Father. Forgive Us. As We forgive. Lead Us. Deliver Us.

I can't live in a world void of grammar forever. Even though it is invigorating. I can get there easily on a foggy hilltop with beagles singing in the valley. I may look "spaced out," "checked out," or "in a zone," but I have abandoned the grammar of power in those moments. Even if for a brief time. There are plenty of other ways. I've done the same while picking blackberries, fishing, playing my mountain dulcimer, or even lying down on the cool cement floor in the basement on a hot summer day. Or staring at a candle when the power goes out at night after a thunderstorm. Sitting on a chair with a dog by my side.

A temporary break from the burden of words is what contemplative prayer does for me. Then, when the words come back, as they necessarily must, I can seek to limit I and magnify We. It's we and us and no longer I and me and mine. I submit my words to the Eternal Word of God. The words of creation, and allow God's Word to fix my grammar. My grammar has the subject all wrong. God's Word has it right.

Oooh. And it's the rest of that prayer. "Hallowed be Thy name" and "Thy kingdom come." Among other things. When the words come back, I must be aware that God's name is Hallowed. God is holy.

And lastly, I must pray, "Thy will be done on earth as it is in heaven." Hmm. The implication is that something ain't right. At least not in this world. It's not like heaven since God's will is not being done. I suspect a huge part of that problem is the Billions of us living lives as the subject and treating the entirety of creation, including humanity, as objects that are either potentially useful or just plain in the way. "Our Father . . ."

I'm gonna go run dogs. Good morning.

Dog

P*roskuneo* **is the** Greek word for worship and literally means "to dog." It is a reference to this position and the position of homage that we often call prostrate. As in "Let angels prostrate fall." Now, some of you will have "All Hail the Power of Jesus's Name" stuck in your head.

The word can also be intended to mean kissing the hand. We've all seen that happen with a dog. Worship is an intentional act of submission to God's will.

A fully trained dog is a pleasure to own. The dog that is obedient and does what it is supposed to do. I've hunted with half-trained dogs. They do not come when called. They chase the wrong critters. The list goes on. When someone brings a half-trained dog, it can make for a long day. Non-sporting dogs also can be fully trained or partially trained.

A good dog can accomplish so much and does so by submitting its own will to the master. And using its talents to do good things. It's not being a mindless robot. I've watched dogs solve tricky things that a rabbit had done. Run 50 yards, then go back on his tracks 30 yards. Pause. And make a huge jump to the side. The dog is looking for the scent trail at the end of the 50 yards and has to think for itself to solve this dilemma.

In Maine, I heard dogs struggling to smell a hare. I was listening and wondering what was happening and saw the hare hopping from rock to rock. Rocks don't hold scent near as well as vegetation or even bare dirt. A couple of dogs figured this out and were looking for rocks and having to get what little scent was there. What I heard was a pack doing well. Then not so much. Then well again. When the hare ran out of rocks, the pursuit sped up with more dogs barking. When more rocks were available, the chase slowed again.

I had one dog in my life that remembered where a rabbit was. He would chase a rabbit and sometimes cross another rabbit's scent trail. I could always tell when this happened. I would shoot a rabbit, and the dog would turn around and go back to where he smelled the other bunny and start a new chase.

Submitting your will to the divine master isn't about losing your identity or personhood. But it does mean doing what the master wants us to do and allowing our passion to be what the master wants. My dogs love chasing rabbits. They need to be obedient. When they are chasing in the non-hunting season, I want them to get on their bellies when I say, "Down!" It's time to go when I say so. And they will get to do it again, probably the next day!

Come. Down. Leave it. With me (my kinda sorta "heel" command), which means to search with me since I think I know the general location of a rabbit.

Being obedient keeps a dog from danger. Porcupines. Roads. Getting lost. I can think of times when my will is definitely subordinated, allowing me to do God's will. Sometimes I find my will rising. I think this can be a particular problem for pastors. We lead, and we can sometimes mistake what we want to do with what God wants. I mean, the pastor is doing church work. So, the pastor must be wanting what God wants.

Maybe. Or maybe the pastor wants what is good for the pastor. Status. A bigger congregation. Compliments. Recognition. Prestige. In seminary, I interviewed for an assistant position at a church in Mansfield, Ohio. I went to worship. The pastor felt he was a genius. The church had a spaghetti dinner after worship. Pastor took me to a different lunch. To an Olive Garden. He refused to eat with the congregation, insulted their cooking, and went for what he considered good Italian food. I turned the job down. It was part-time and paid 12K per year. That was a lot of money for a seminarian in the 1990s. He was a pastor who taught me some things not to do. Including feeling that he was smarter than the people he served. "I won't dumb down sermons for them. Have you read Wesley's sermons?"

Of course, I read them. And they weren't preached. There was an established genre of sermons meant to be read, often by clergy and church leaders. So, this pastor wasn't as educated as he thought. In more subtle ways, it is easy to exert our will instead of God's will. I've recycled old sermons on weeks I've been busy doing things I've wanted to do. My sermons are written as outlines with very few words. Because I write them on Saturday night, I don't need much of a memory jog for a biblical text I have been living with all week. When I dust that outline off several years later, the outline doesn't help as much as I want. I haven't worked with the verses all week like I usually do. All because I spent too much time doing my will during the week. I've officiated weddings for strangers and not cared to do it. When I get asked to bury someone without a church, I have a stock sermon for funerals. I may not want to go to the visiting hours at the funeral home the day before and learn something about the deceased because I want to do something else. I'm not even close to perfect.

It's almost Christmas. I'm trying to be a well-trained dog. I hope I'm not exerting my will like a half-trained dog. I don't want to focus on being the popular gift giver. I don't want to dread seeing in-laws. I don't want to spend too much money. But, at least to some degree, I do.

All dogs have lapses in obedience. Let angels prostrate fall. Old guys talk about their prostrates instead of their prostates. One is a movement. The other is a gland that gives you trouble as you age. At the job interview, I remember that pastor bad-mouthing an old guy for saying prostrate.

But why did he say it? Why prostRate instead of prostate? Because the guy had lived in his bible and hymnal. And read prostrate and sung prostrate countless times. I'm going "to dog" and be obedient. And that means living in my Bible and singing my faith.

Bob Ford

Law and Morality

It's tough to get ten commandments out of the Ten Commandments. Well, not really, but sort of. Protestants & Orthodox have a different list than Roman Catholics. We Prots start with:

1. I am the Lord your God; you shall have no other God before me.
2. You shall not make any carved images.

Our Catholic brothers and sisters combine those two into one; then they will separate the prohibition against coveting into two commands:

9. Don't covet your neighbor's wife.
10. Don't covet your neighbor's house.

Protestants have 10. Don't covet.

The Jewish Decalogue is mostly like the Protestant version, except it goes:

1. I am the Lord your God
2. You shall have no other gods before me. Do not make any carved images.

See that slight difference? They are the oldest tradition of this.

Anyway, in my youth, I felt that the Roman Catholic system did two things—allowed for all those beautiful statues because the prohibition against idols was minimized by being absorbed into the command to have no other Gods—and secondly, fed the thoughts of celibate leaders by dividing the command not to covet into two commands, one of which was not to covet your neighbor's wife. The other was not to covet everything else. Singling out the wife as an object of coveting seemed overly sexualized.

Then again, maybe that system is better as it sees women as more than property. Let's face it, marriage law and property law seem a little too similar in the ancient world. Maybe the highlighting of wife coveting is humanizing. The history of Western Civilization doesn't bear that out, but the seeds are there. I'm not as critical of my Roman Catholic sisters and brothers now.

That's a long intro to my main theological ramble this morning. We can't even agree on what the Big Ten are. Ha! I snuck that in for the football fans. Get it? There are more than ten teams in the Big Ten. Just like the Commandments could be seen to have more than ten. Ahem. Ok. Not all jokes work . . .

So if the really major laws cannot find consensus, what hope is there for the rest? There are 613 commands within the Torah in the tradition of Judaism. No, I can't name them all.

This has always been a problem. Throughout the history of the church, movements of antinomianism have sporadically popped up. That's just a fancy word for anti-law. The early Gnostics were indifferent or at least tolerant of sexual sin. Marcion rejected the entire Old Testament. At the beginning of Protestantism, some emphasized the Gospel and grace to the point where the law seemed irrelevant and not binding.

Granted, I don't think any of those groups intended to create an environment that could become an incubator for sin, but the celebration of faith and the neglect of works, the preaching of the gospel without reminding us that the gospel frees us from sin; well it gets complicated and could lead to a view that sin was no more. Defeated. Grace abounds. So why list laws?

Bramble Rambles

Paul can be complicated. In Romans 7:7, he tells us that he learned sin from the law. You can read through the Exodus-Deuteronomy and find sins listed that never occurred to you. When I was a teenager, my friends and I were going to go camping. I had to get permission. I approached my dad. He had already raised my older half-siblings.

"You aren't gonna get some 21-year-old loser to buy beer, are you?" He asked.

"No."

"You aren't going to have girls show up that all lie to their parents about being at a sleepover at one of the girl's houses, are you?" He asked.

"No."

"Okay then."

When my friends asked me what my father said, I replied, "He said yes. And he had a couple of good ideas that we missed . . ."

In some ways, the law can aid us in sinning. Want to cheat on your taxes? Read the tax code. Those laws are written because someone DID what they said not to do. Read those laws, and you can find loopholes. That's what corporate lawyers and accountants do for a living. They find a way to follow the letter of the law and be unethical.

I think Paul helps us here. In Romans 10:4, he says that Christ is the *telos* of the law. That little Greek word often gets translated as "end." But that should be more like the end, as in ends and means. In fact, the word also means goal.

Oh, I think that's the meaning here. Christ is the goal of the law. He wasn't a legalistic messiah looking for loopholes like a tax accountant. He healed on the Sabbath. He interacted with sinners. He let unclean people touch him, and he touched them. He saw the law as something to benefit the human community. That's it, isn't it? It's not about using the law to justify my desires or control your actions. It's not about singular people; even though we all are responsible for our actions, it is about OUR community under God. Not me and he and she, but we and us.

If he is the goal, then we can also be the goal. That's because of the Spirit of Christ that dwells within us. I doubt that many have read this far. So I will leave you with this:

Bob Ford

Squabbling about the Supreme Court appointment always seems weird to me. By the time anything gets to the Supreme Court, things have been severely broken within the community of us and we. The Supreme Court denied citizenship to African American slaves (*Dred Scott*) and ended the segregation that made less quality schools for black people (*Brown vs. Board of Education*). By the time anything gets to that body, we have a societal problem. Whether the court is moral or immoral has much to do with the laws that Congress passes. Laws that the court follows. Morality rests within the community of God. All else, very often, left and right, is the pursuit of loopholes for personal gain.

Sure, they killed Jesus for properly seeing the law as the foundation for loving each other in the community. Healing even on the Sabbath. Contact with a bleeding woman to heal her. Raising a dead girl to life by touching the child (that's why the Samaritan is the hero in that story Jesus told. The Levite and priest did not want to risk touching a guy who might be dead. They would be unclean if they did). Morality starts in our house and our church.

Homecoming

The prodigal son. That's what we call the parable, but it might better be called the parable of the obedient son. It's the good son that has the problem. I call the people like the good son "congenital Christians." They might feel like they've always been a believer. They've been in church their whole lives.

And they mistakenly think that a life of sin, outside of grace, is fun. They are being good and working hard. The sinners, the good brothers, can think and are having fun. They (the fun-loving sinners) might make a deathbed conversion. And the good son will be resentful. Because he thinks the little brother had a fun-filled sinful time and then returned out of desperation. Living outside of grace may look like fun in a secular world, but if you truly talk to people, you will find it isn't so.

When the father celebrated the return of the younger son, who squandered his inheritance, a party was thrown. The good son resented this.

Grace is a powerful thing. Transformative. And some believers recognize this power and have decided it's too much to offer to anyone. Some churches decided to limit this grace. In fact, many are taught that the atonement offered by Christ is limited.

Now, I'm a Wesleyan, and in our tradition, it is believed that Christ died for all. Granted, not everyone claims that is offered salvation, but we can choose Christ.

An alternative is found in some Calvinistic traditions. The emphasis is that if hell exists, then someone is going there. God has chosen who will be with him and who will not. It's limited atonement, just for the elect. This is the heart of predestination. It has been predetermined where you will go. In radical forms, you can't decide where you are headed. And in some teaching, you can't know if you have been saved. You can live your whole life and never be secure in your faith. The $64 term for knowing you are saved is Assurance. As in the hymn "Blessed Assurance." And now it is stuck in your head too.

I think (and many people much smarter than me in the history of Christianity also say so) that grace is not limited. We don't have to compete for God's Grace. Like when the local grocery has a sale not listed in the paper, and limited purchase applies. And people call their relatives, "Betty, get down here. Crescent rolls are on sale; buy one, get one free. Limit four per person. I can't buy more than four! Get down here!"

Nah. Grace is immense. Hell is not a place God wants anyone to go. There is more than enough grace; we just have to accept it. I'll go one step further . . .

People say they are glad the roof didn't fall down in the church because they haven't been there in years or decades. Perhaps, like the prodigal, they have been outside grace and experienced that it is not fun. It's brokenness when you are away. And they return to God.

So, I always say the same thing. I say, "Of course, the roof is fine. I come here every week. Of course, the church is good for you. More importantly, you are good for the church. A reminder of grace. The good things of grace. A corrective lens to the myopic vision of the pretty good people who don't see sin accurately. People who judge your foray away, your bad trip, your broken and battered return to faith and see only your sinful past. And fail to see the less colossal but much more insidious sin in their own life. The son that would rather rejoice at the failure of his prodigal brother than rejoice at his redemption is in peril."

Blessings to you. And the fatted calf and party await your return. If we cannot extend grace, I dare say we never received it.

Earthly Good

Ahh. Karl Marx. Big shot philosopher. Wrote about the working class freeing themselves from oppression. He was an upper-middle-class guy and never really lived the life of the working poor. He did much of his writing far off from the working poor in a museum in England. He was a Prussian (northern Germany), but his writing had more influence in Russia. The communists loved his stuff.

Marx called religion "The opiate of the people." Now, we live in an opioid crisis in our times, and you could be forgiven if you felt that Marx meant that religion was addictive. That's not what he meant. Opium was to alleviate pain then, particularly for the dying.

He criticized religion because he felt that religion helped people dull the pain of life and accept the status quo. In other words, he felt that Christianity made people accept poverty and be content because they knew the reward for faith was eternal life. Religion numbed people to accept terrible lives in return for heavenly citizenship after death.

Here's the thing. He may have been right. By that, I mean he may have encountered that message from churches. Churches can sometimes forget all that stuff Jesus said. Some famous Christian, whose name eludes me, said, "Don't become so heavenly-minded that you are no earthly good." Sometimes Christians are no earthly good.

Bob Ford

Christmas is all about baby Jesus coming here to upset things. Like he upset those tables in the temple right before they killed him. Christmas is about the working poor (shepherds) first hearing good news. Christmas is about the last being first.

I'm no Marxist. I'm no communist. But, what gripes me is that Marx had to get his ideas because he saw Christians actually doing things to allow suffering by promising an afterlife. We've always been called to improve things in this world. Our king was born in a feed trough. Not a palace.

Radical Equality

Hymns are catchy. In other words, they help us remember words. Many scholars view Philippians 2:5-11 as part of a hymn; we just don't know the music. Just like we don't know the music that goes with the psalms.

In that Philippians text, Paul says:

> 5 Let this mind be in you which was also in Christ Jesus, 6 who, being in the form of God, did not consider it [a]robbery to be equal with God, 7 but [b]made Himself of no reputation, taking the form of a bondservant, and coming in the likeness of men. 8 And being found in appearance as a man, He humbled Himself and became obedient to the point of death, even the death of the cross. 9 Therefore God also has highly exalted Him and given Him the name which is above every name, 10 that at the name of Jesus every knee should bow, of those in heaven, and of those on earth, and of those under the earth, 11 and that every tongue should confess that Jesus Christ is Lord, to the glory of God the Father.

We have a hymn commonly known today with part of this passage. "Every knee shall bow, and tongue confess, that Jesus Christ is Lord." And now it's stuck in your head too. Paul says that the divinity took the form of a slave. Bondservant in that translation. Some estimates claim that forty percent of the population in Italy was comprised of slaves. In further flung reaches of the empire, the percentage was lower, but make no mistake; all ancient economies were slavery based.

And if you were not a slave, you were still very obligated in a society that was keenly aware of status. Complex patron-client relationships kept order in Roman society. The aristocrats were patrons. The more land and wealth they had, the more power and clients. If a slave gained freedom, he became a client of his former owner. He doesn't really escape. Freeborn people could choose their patron and even change patrons. Clients reported at dawn to their patron to honor him. Clients did the heavy lifting of any task. Patrons were obliged to provide legal counsel and provide food for clients.

A patron could be a client to a more powerful patron. A client could acquire a few clients and be a patron to them. So, you could be both a patron and a client. "Don't patronize me" is a phrase we use to show when we are being used. It's a system that serves the top. And there is nothing like the upward mobility that we can enjoy today.

And into this culture, Paul writes that God became a slave in the form of Jesus. Slaves are below all clients. No Roman god of any power would do that.

People certainly knew where they stood. But there were constant reminders, for instance, at public meals. Imagine if you went to a wedding with four different meals, depending on who you were. Prime rib for the bride and groom. Pot roast for the wedding party. Chicken for the family. Fish sticks for the rest.

When patrons held feasts, it was like that. Your status was on display, on your plate. Slaves, of course, were at the bottom.

The Passover is a meal rooted in the escape from slavery. The first Passover meal was eaten right before liberation from 400 years of slavery in Egypt. The last supper was a Passover meal. In the church, it gets transformed into the Eucharist, or holy communion, and served every week. The early church had no large public buildings. They met in church members' homes. Often one of the bigger houses, for obvious reasons. Oooh, that person might be a patron in society. You can guess where I am going next.

Paul's letters talk about problems around meals. In the early church, Eucharist accompanied a full meal. And early on, it was resolved that everyone would eat the same food. Bread, the same meal, then the wine to finish the sacrament.

As the church moved into larger, public spaces, the sacrament became bread and wine only. But can you imagine the overwhelming statement that was conveyed at a meal at that time when everyone was made equal? Equality in Christ, the slave. The Passover meal celebrating escaping slavery transformed into a sacrament that proclaimed equality. If like me, you will attend a Maundy Thursday service tomorrow, that divine equality is built into the sacrament we will share. No patron, just God and brothers and sisters in Christ.

Guilt and Shame

Guilt and shame are two different entities that can surface and subside and re-emerge again throughout our lives. Guilt is, in many ways, a legal pronouncement. This may have shame associated with it. Who knows, maybe not. Ever talk to someone who brags about their transgressions? Not only is there no shame, there is almost a pride that accompanies the guilt. Especially if the guilt has no ramifications. The person gets away with it.

"Man, I topped out at 110 mph on that stretch of road."

"I shot that deer on ground posted 'No Trespassing' but got out of there before anyone noticed."

"The waitress forgot to bill us for half of our food. Oh well, their mistake. Their loss."

Speeding, trespassing, and theft. Those are all laws. And we haven't even mentioned divine laws that are not in our state or federal law code. Like the command that we not covet. Or commands from that rabble-rouser Jesus who tells us to love our enemies and turn the other cheek.

Suffice it to say that we have all sinned and felt no shame. This is especially true when no one knows. When we are jealous but don't act on it. When we are angry and spiteful towards a person, but only when that person isn't present. When it's been a long day, and I decide to give in to my gluttonous urges and eat the whole dang pizza. These things have no stigma in society. We can sin, and boldly so, and have no shame.

Shame comes when our sin gets to be on public display. When embezzlement happens at the local nonprofit and the whole world knows. If an affair gets discovered. A DUI. Here we have guilt with shame.

Now, I started with guilt without shame. That has its own problems. In a life of faith, that means that the believer clearly has not realized that we are always caught by God, even if society doesn't care about the particular sin that we do. That problem is real. But I want to talk about the flip side of that coin. Shame without guilt.

People can suffer shame and embarrassment even when they are without guilt. No sin. Just a couple of oddball things that happened to me: I get up early. In the winter, I will get dressed in the dark not to wake my wife. I once did that, drove a long way to visit a church member at a hospital, and discovered that I was wearing one brown shoe and one black shoe. There is no sin in this. I can't describe how ashamed and embarrassed I felt. And there was no reason to feel that way. I once threw my clothes in the dryer on Sunday morning to remove wrinkles. Probably some dog hair too. During the prelude, I walked down the center aisle of the church to begin worship with a washcloth static clung to my backside. No sin. But the shame was there.

Some people walk in chronic shame though they are not guilty. A guy who gets laid off because of economic machinations, and he is crushed because of a perception that he isn't providing. A victim of domestic abuse who is living with the guilty party but is not guilty of anything. She feels shame even though the guilt belongs to her husband or boyfriend. I remember kids that qualified for free lunch in school used these paper tickets instead of giving money. Some hid the ticket in the palm of their hand and gave it discreetly to the attendant. Ashamed. And no guilt was present. Victims of sexual assault who feel shame for the sin that violated them. They were victims, not sinners. The person who goes bankrupt paying medical bills and loses a home and has to move in with relatives.

Bramble Rambles

Again, no guilt. The kid that gets bullied, their self-esteem crushed, who is ashamed and unhappy and feels (incorrectly) unworthy.

You can see chronic shame. People who hang their heads. Avert their eyes. They remain isolated. They can't stand to be seen. Avoid public places, sometimes. And they have done nothing wrong.

The shameless sinner? I'm concerned about that. We need to make the world aware of sin. But I feel we are all called to help the sinless shamed. Victims ought not to feel guilty, and they should not feel powerless. Their power can come from Christ, and it may arrive at their heart in the form of the Holy Spirit that dwells in you and me.

Vanity

Qoheleth. The preacher or teacher in Hebrew. Usually, it is left as the Greek translation, Ecclesiastes, in most Christian Bibles. It is the book in the Bible right after proverbs.

It starts: "The words of the Teacher, the son of David, king in Jerusalem.

Vanity of vanities, says the Teacher, vanity of vanities! All is vanity."

Vanity is the translation of the NRSV. A more accurate translation might be meaningless. The Hebrew is *hevel*. It means vapor. Or breath. It's fleeting, and you can't grasp it. Ultimately, Ecclesiastes concludes that this is the nature of our lives. We are here and then gone. Within a couple of generations, we are forgotten. If you've ever traced your genealogy, it doesn't take long until you are researching total strangers. Generations come and go. The future is unseen by us.

The author of Ecclesiastes sees all that we do as meaningless. He worked to be successful in life, and even that is ultimately *hevel*. In 8:15, the preacher advocates that we enjoy life. "Then I commended mirth, because a man hath no better thing under the sun, than to eat, and to drink, and to be merry." This isn't hedonism, where you live a life of debauchery to numb yourself against the pain of this world, but rather it is the acknowledgment that we can find joy in the here and now while we also admit that our lives will be gone and forgotten.

Ultimately, the good and the sinful find the same end. Death. No matter how we live, that's the end game.

I remember riding on the school bus in elementary school. The bus was so loud you could hardly talk to each other. I'd rest my head against the window and stare at the trees on the side of the road. Letting things get blurry and feeling the RPMs of the engine vibrate the entire bus. And I remember thinking, "If I was never born, it wouldn't change this day. The bus would still be doing this trip. Or, if I was born someone else, it wouldn't much matter either. If some other family lived in my house, then some other kid would be in this seat. We have to get on this bus, go to school, and follow rules."

I should confess that I wasn't a fan of going to school. I missed being outside. I felt like I was just a cog in a system. In kindergarten, I did okay. First grade was all day long. It took three adults to squeeze me through the door of the bus the first two weeks. I howled like a wounded animal. Later, after going to college and seminary, my gram said, "Couldn't get you to go to school at first. Now you won't stop."

Qoheleth is dealing with the reality that we are, by and large, subject to forces greater than ourselves, and life is, by and large, filled with anonymity. What do I mean by that?

I remember going on a field trip to Penn State as a kid. 40,000 plus students. We were in a science building, having gone to see the Earth and Mineral Science labs. We saw a paleontology class with students slicing fossilized rock to look at tiny organisms from ancient oceans. It was a night class, and when we were waiting to leave, I looked out the window and down at the busy street below. Dimly lit sidewalks. Cars whooshing by. Students moving everywhere. I thought, "I know none of them. I never would. They don't know each other, for the most part."

And I guess that's life. Mostly disjointed and unconnected lives, briefly encountering each other as we go about our days. But in my own life, I can have my own influence on the people important to me. Eat. Drink. Be merry.

Bramble Rambles

Ecclesiastes is one of my favorite books of the Bible. Maybe my favorite Old Testament book. My wife reminded me today that I often say, "Without Jesus, all we got is Ecclesiastes."

Jesus, on the other hand, bursts into our lives. Remember me looking down at those students bustling along in autonomous anonymity of life? If I could have speedily become friends with them all, forged a common friendship, then we would all be connected rather than each plodding on separate paths to the same dirt destination. That's ludicrous, me quickly befriending 40,000 students.

Prior to Christ, I think of God looking at all the lives of humanity similarly. Of course, God knew them all, even if they didn't know each other. Or him. Generation after Generation.

Then, that physical, fleshy Jesus changed everything. And the gift of the Holy Spirit changed it even more. The Spirit allows Christ to connect to each believer. And if you are connected to Christ, and I am connected to Christ, then you and I are connected. Even if we don't know each other. And we are both also connected to Him and her and them. All of that forms a massive we. "WE" encompass all geography and all generations.

Ecclesiastes says that we can form our own small, insular, nepotistic "us" and try to find meaning against the vast "them." That's the best we can do without Christ. Eat, drink, be Merry, and enjoy the ride. However long it lasts.

With Christ, our small "us" becomes the massive "WE," and "them" is really people waiting for the connective Christ that transforms them into part of the ever-growing "WE." The body of Christ. WE work for the Kingdom and can also eat and drink and be merry, enjoying the ride that never ends.

Acts and Money

Two stories in the Book of Acts indicate what drew negative attention and growth to the church in the New Testament Times. One is Acts 16. Paul encounters a slave girl possessed by a spirit that lets her predict the future. Paul casts out the spirit, and she can no longer work as a fortune teller. Her owners lose money. Paul and his companions are beaten and imprisoned. God frees them.

In Acts 19, Paul has been evangelizing and convincing people in Ephesus to give up false gods and the idols associated with those false gods. The silversmiths, who make their livelihood by selling those idols, create a mob and riot in protest about not making the money they once did. Or maybe it is a concern that they would not make money in the future as more and more people followed Christ. Paul flees to Macedonia.

Disrupting the local economy is what gets noticed by the authorities. More so than the beliefs of Christians. In a world with no refrigeration or canning, many people bought meat at the Temple. Critters got sacrificed there. Temples were also butcher shops. You could not preserve a whole cow, but you could buy part of one. Or goat. Or whatever. This is why meat was often associated with feasts in the Old Testament. You invited enough people to eat it all.

Many Christians stopped getting meat at the pagan temples because they knew meat was sacrificed to some other god. The same would have been true for wine. Some believers felt it was okay to eat that meat since they knew the gods did not exist. 1 Corinthians 8 is all about this tension. Not buying meat drew attention from the outside too.

All that negative attention from the powers that be helped the church grow. It never hurt them. The beliefs behind what Christians did appeal to others. Attracted new believers.

What if we did the same today? It's safe to say that the business world sees Christmas as a chance to make a glut of money. I have known people compelled to give their kids a "good Christmas" and get the credit card paid off the following November. In time to do it again. I'm not opposed to gifts, but it could be done responsibly and meaningfully. If we shopped differently at Christmas, we would draw attention. "Fourth quarter profits are not booming . . ." the news would say. And talk about Christians refusing to commercialize Christmas.

I remember reading about a church that studied the food prices of the grocery stores in town. They bought the same staples every week. They found that the prices went up on the first week of the month. That's when people on assistance get funds designated for food. That's also when senior citizens got their social security checks too, or at least back then. Now the date for receiving social security checks is staggered throughout the month. The church I was serving in seminary decided to do the same. For all the stores in town. One was much higher the first week. We put flyers up in public places. I got a call from a grocery store manager. He changed their policy. We took the signs down. But we kept monitoring the prices.

Predatory loans, new "electric companies" that offer a short-term lower rate followed rapidly by an exorbitant longer-term price for kilowatt hours, and other scams come to mind. Do I know the details about how we can fix these abusive matters? No. Maybe we need to be beaten and jailed. Prison has been a good finishing school, from the Apostle Paul to Martin Luther King Jr. I know that what we do with money matters. A great deal.

Born Again

I never had children of my own. On a couple of occasions, I have held a newborn. First of all, no one told me what color that first bowel movement would be. I mean, wow. Now that I think about it, a warning probably wouldn't have helped.

Secondly, I have never heard a more unhappy sound in my life. That crying from emerging into the world. If the baby had words, they would say, "I was so happy where I was. Why did you bring me out here?"

The light must be utterly astonishing. The temperature change. The first sensation of cold. And hunger. Going from complete bliss to utter misery.

None of us remember our birth. If you ask your adult kid if they remember being born, of course, the answer is no. No memory at all of prenatal life.

But if you ask me if I want to return to the womb, I would tell you absolutely not. After the sudden burst of misery at birth, life is amazing. All the experiences, adventures, journeys, and memories. All the firsts. First bite of a favorite food. First time riding a bike. For me, my first successful hunt. First kiss, first car, first home.

All the friendships. All those people that you are connected to in various ways. If you are like me, you have friends in completely different circles. My church friends do not all associate with my deer hunting friends, and they aren't familiar with the friends from beagling. Then there are friends separated by time and space. As we age and move with work, we get new friends. I have childhood friends, friends from college, others from seminary, and friends from each parish I have served. Some circles of friends have nothing in common with others.

And that all contributes to the life we live, which will end. This brings me back to that wailing newborn. We have no memory of our birth or the misery that accompanied it. Or life in the womb.

The Bible gives little description of the afterlife while giving a lot of references. Jesus prepares a place for us; there will be no tears, streets of gold, the tree of life, worship, and bliss.

Eternity is an overwhelming concept, and I wonder if the afterlife will be such that we will have no recollection of this life we live now, just as we currently do not recall birth. All those memories of firsts that I mentioned above might fade away. But so would pain. Loss. Grief. The emotional swamp that floods us when we are reminded of a tragedy. Maybe if you see a car like the one a friend drove until a car wreck took his life. Ever wake yourself from a dream because dead loved ones are in it, and you realize it must be a dream?

I've watched people die. Been in the room. It's an occupational part of the vocational choice I've made. The death rattle breathing is the worst. A family that has to decide to take away life support is a very difficult thing to see. I've lost people suddenly too. No time for goodbyes or final "I love you." Just a phone call telling you that someone you love has died.

I like to think that eternity will be so awesome (an overused word if there ever was one) that we will not remember this world's trials, failures, pain, and loss. Just as we don't remember the misery of being born. We will be with loved ones, all those circles of friends that will be one great circle. Unbroken circle, I'll put that hymn in your noggin. And we won't be waking ourselves up because we know those dead relatives can't interact with us, the living. We will all be there as the resurrected, knowing that if it seems too good to be true, it is heaven. And that's the ultimate truth.

Looking for Kind Faith

A few years ago, I was watching *Game of Thrones* with some people. I watched the show for a couple of seasons until it got to be too much effort to remember the plots and storylines. I'm not that serious about any show.

"I've been there," I said as the show depicted a city.

"That's a movie set." Someone said, "The city of King's Landing isn't real."

"That is Dubrovnik," I said, "And it's very real. A medieval city on the Adriatic Sea."

I was there in 1984. I was twelve years old and had won a trip to Italy and Yugoslavia through my paper route, the *Erie Sunday Times*. Before its sale not too long ago, it was the county's oldest family-owned paper. Anyway, the trip was sponsored by *Parade Magazine*. Remember that? *Parade* was part of the Sunday paper. Part of the "guts." The guts—*Parade*, coupons, advertisements, and other inserts arrived at my house on Wednesday, tucked inside the comic strips. The rest arrived at about 3 a.m. Sunday morning, landing with a thud on the front porch. The noise woke the house, and assembly began for over 100 papers. Open the newly arrived news, remove the guts from the comics, shove them into the center of the news sections, and put the comics around the paper as a cover. This was when papers were thicker, and a news carrier bag could hold about twenty.

The Winter Olympics were in Sarajevo in 1984, and our visit sent us there afterward. *Parade* paid half. The *Erie Times* paid half. I won a contest. We were there for Palm Sunday and Easter. The Iron Curtain still stood, and Soviet soldiers with AK-47s followed us everywhere. I was the youngest kid there, barely making the minimum age of twelve.

I saw the soldiers. I understood what that was. I did not know that a seething tension was invisible to me and in plain sight to the people who lived there. The Catholic Croatians, Serbian Orthodox, and Bosnian Muslims lived with religious and ethnic differences that caused real hatred.

All three groups disliked each other. It wasn't strictly Christian versus Muslim. It was also Orthodox versus Catholic. The 20th Century began in the Balkans with an assassination in Sarajevo that ignited WWI. It ended with genocide in the same region.

It never ceases to surprise me how people who profess faith in Christ can be filled with anger and hate. And not just in extreme measures like genocide. It's the active church member that glares at a young mother on Sunday because the baby is crying. That church member may say, "My kids didn't do that." Of course, her kids did.

I cringe on Easter when someone inevitably says, "It is good to see everyone here today. Hope you keep coming." That almost guarantees that some of them will not—they've just been insulted in a passive-aggressive way.

In Matthew 8, the Roman Centurion comes to Jesus and says he has a servant that needs to be healed. Jesus does it. From the cross, he asks for forgiveness for his executors. This is the enemy. Rome was brutal. I struggle with Jesus helping them. The goal is always to bring people, even the enemy, to Christ. The person we don't like at work, the annoying neighbor across the street, the relative you had a dispute with over money, the friend that has not talked to you in years over an argument. Our goal should always be to love and witness to Christ. No matter what, we are called to Love. No group of people should be viewed with disdain because of their ancestry or religion. Yugoslavia is now many smaller countries, but what happened there could happen anywhere.

Spring Break. 1993. I worked at the library on campus. Didn't go anywhere. Feet of snow fell. Nothing was open in State College, Pennsylvania. Penn State was shut down. There was a place called Pennsylvania Pizza, and it had a bar called John Henry's. It was the only place open, at least close to where I lived. For several days people in the area who could walk through waist-deep snow lived on food there. Cold pizza and warm beer were the daily menu.

A student from Turkey and another from Ireland were sitting with me one day. One of my majors was religious studies, and I was doing some homework as I had lunch. Neither was a fan of religion. Ireland is a case study of what Christians can do to each other. The Turkish student was all too familiar with troubles and conflict when different faiths interact. Both students were opposed to a belief in God.

If practicing our faith causes people to give up on their belief in God, we are doing it wrong. This whole ramble started because I saw an adult delivering newspapers with a car this morning on my way to run dogs; kids don't seem to have paper routes. Newspapers are thinner and thinner. I'm thinking about the seething tensions in our own country. And the violence directly opposes the Christ that prayed for his enemies as He died on the cross.

Compassion

I try and sometimes fail to take Jesus seriously. Discipleship baffles the secular partisans. Some think I'm a callous conservative because my thinking embraces the concept of original sin. A sin that goes to the core of humanity and makes us sin on purpose. Disciples understand that a modern approach of "You can do whatever you want as long as you aren't hurting anyone else" is not enough. We were never commanded not to hurt our neighbor but rather to love our neighbor. Hedonistic do-as-you-please live for pleasure only isn't our toolkit.

And that leads me to times when the secular world or even the ecclesiastical world will accuse a disciple of being a liberal. Churches get requests for money. Sometimes they are scams. I've been scammed a couple of times, though I try to be careful. We never give money. I'll make a payment on a bill. Even one that is currently paid to free up cash for other things. Sometimes a rainy day happens. Illness strikes. Employers cut back on the number of employees. Sometimes all the planning goes awry, and people are in a pinch. Often people donate back to the helping hand fund later. More frequently, they don't. But we don't help with that expectation.

I once lived where the local clergy ministerium had a fund to help people, separate from each of our churches. We received a request for a winter coat one year for a girl who had outgrown her coat. Oh yeah, she was very heavy too. She couldn't zip her coat, and kids at the bus stop teased her.

"Does this kid go to any of our churches?" was asked, and the answer was that she did not. "Who cares? She needs a coat, and it is winter," was my response.

"I understand the need," a pastor continued, "Maybe the kid needs to diet."

"Gimme the family contact info," I said, "I'll buy the damn coat and deliver it."

The fact that I said "damn" was the most problematic issue in the room. Not the indifference with which we were discussing a kid standing in the cold without a coat because she got teased for being overweight. "Damn" wasn't the word that was in my mind either; it was the big daddy bomb.

"Cheap, affordable food isn't low calorie, high fiber, and nutritious. It's noodles. Potatoes. We all know what it is. And if this kid has parents that squandered the family income, that isn't her fault." I said that. Or something like that.

We paid for the coat and a clergyman present at the time called me a liberal. It is just as inaccurate as when you call me a conservative. I don't follow a donkey or an elephant. I follow a Lion from the tribe of Judah. Discipleship has nothing to do with liberal or conservative.

Dangerous Faith

Ever notice that your best stories are about lived moments that were perhaps not pleasant when you were living those moments? A pleasant day at the beach doesn't make as good of a story as the time you got stung by the jellyfish or the person that survived a shark attack.

Ever endured someone talking about how great their supper was at the restaurant last weekend? That story is never as intriguing as the guy that comes to work on Monday with a story of getting bad food on Friday night and spending the weekend near the bathroom.

Paul lists his misery in 2 Corinthians 11. Starting in verse 16. Hunger. Thirst. Nakedness and cold. Shipwrecks. Jail time. Whippings. Beating with rods. Angry mobs in cities. Dangerous people while traveling in rural places. It is quite a list. Sleeplessness.

One of my mentors in faith, Tom, who has passed away, was in Sierra Leone during the civil war. He was part of a mission trip that dug water wells for communities lacking water. One night, they were surrounded by armed militia. They did not hurt any mission workers but stole the well casings to make mortars for combat.

Someone from the parish where I serve had a son who did a lot of mission work. He was in Haiti already doing ministry when the deadly earthquake of 2010 struck. He died in the earthquake.

I'm not saying that everyone should seek out life-threatening situations. But the church is called to more than potlucks and concerts. For the record, I love potlucks and concerts. A lot.

I always say that working with the poor is scary. You may think it could be contagious. Most of us would be in trouble if we missed a paycheck. It's tough to realize that the thing that separates "us" from "them" is one paycheck. Our Vacation Bible School kids donated all the collected money from the week for the school backpack program. The kids who qualify for the backpacks leave school on Friday with food for the weekend. In other words, school lunches are their best meal of the week for them.

A few weeks ago, we buried a church member who died in a nursing home. A nursing home that she and her husband visited every week to do visits with the residents there. Not comfortable ministry. You are confronted by mortality every time you go. A harsh reminder of death, which we rarely think about in the bustle of the daily grind. After decades of volunteering in that home, she entered as a resident. I wonder how often she had visited people in the room where she died.

I drove a '78 FJ-40 for years. Almost two decades ago, fifty-plus UMC churches organized a day of food and fun in Potter County, Pennsylvania. It was in response to the Aryan Nation moving their headquarters there. A way of saying that we were opposed to hate. An FJ-40 sticks out. Weeks later, I come off a stream. I had been trout fishing. A guy was waiting at my vehicle. "You one of them n***** loving Methodists," he asked me.

"Yep," I said and stared him in the eyes. I didn't know what he was gonna do. I was 29. I could throw a lot of weight around then. I'd carry four bags of dog food at a time, 50 lbs each. One on each shoulder, one in each hand. I didn't know what I'd do if the guy started something. He was probably closer to 50 or older. I figured that I could whoop him pretty bad. But I also was thinking about that "turn the other cheek" thing. I could take a punch without fighting back. Maybe two or three. But would I start throwing because I couldn't control myself?

Bramble Rambles

Then I wondered if he had a weapon. Maybe I'd buy the farm right there along the road. He pointed a finger at me, "You're the biggest problem we face as a race," he said. And walked away. I was shaking a bit. I was nervous. It wasn't fun. But, after all the years since then, it's better than any potluck story I have. The world ain't safe. And it's the mission field.

www.ingramcontent.com/pod-product-compliance
Lightning Source LLC
LaVergne TN
LVHW041338080426
835512LV00006B/524